Screening the Beats

Screening the Beats: Media Culture and the Beat Sensibility

David Sterritt

Southern Illinois University Press
Carbondale

Printed in the United States of America
07 06 05 04 4 3 2 1

Library of Congress Cataloging-in-Publication Data
Sterritt, David.
Screening the Beats : media culture and the Beat sensibility / David Sterritt.
p. cm.
Includes bibliographical references and index.
1. American literature—20th century—History and criticism. 2. Beat generation. 3. Mass media and literature—United States—History—20th century. 4. Kerouac, Jack, 1922–1969—Film and video adaptations. 5. Mass media—United States—History—20th century. 6. American literature—Film and video adaptations. I. Title.
PS228.B6 S76 2004
810.9'11—dc21
ISBN 0-8093-2563-2 (alk. paper) 2003013286

Printed on recycled paper. ♻

The paper used in this publication meets the minimum requirements of American National Standard for Information Sciences—Permanence of Paper for Printed Library Materials, ANSI Z39.48-1992. ∞

For M. B.

CONTENTS

PREFACE

It was in 1951 that fledgling novelist Jack Kerouac started hammering out *On the Road,* his first major book. He typed it on sheets of drawing paper taped into a long roll so nothing, absolutely nothing, would interrupt the mercurial flow of what he later called his "spontaneous bop prosody."

Kerouac's improvisational technique proved controversial when Viking finally published the book six years later. The *New York Times* gave it a rave review, instantly placing its unknown author on the cultural map. On the flip side, novelist Truman Capote sniffed that it was "typing," not "writing." The debate grew, and soon culture-conscious Americans were choosing up sides over Kerouac's novel and the loosely knit Beat Generation group that spawned it. The other core members were Allen Ginsberg, a modernist bard influenced by everything from eighteenth-century poet Christopher Smart to the patter of late-night radio talkers, and William S. Burroughs, a radical storyteller with an appetite for drugs, sex, and metaphysics.

The group's influence still lingers. Its rebellious values have waxed and waned in the public imagination, but they have always been in view somewhere on the social horizon, especially among people simultaneously nagged by cultural discontent and skeptical about the efficacy of political activism. Borrowings from the Beats have crept into a long line of latter-day trends, and one theory holds that the cyberpunks of the early twenty-first century are their near-identical twins—ornery loners fending off cooptation by mainstream culture while blazing the trail for more explosive movements to come.

Cinema has capitalized on the Beats and their ilk since the end of the World War II era. Moviegoers were mesmerized when 1950s dramas like *The Wild One* and *Rebel Without a Cause* made disciplined actors like Marlon Brando and James Dean into symbols of an anarchic generation teetering on the brink of revolution against everything in sight. Soon theater and television screens swarmed with beatniks, derisively named after the Beats and Sputnik, the paranoia-producing Soviet satellite launched in 1957. Exploitation films like *Beat Girl* and *A Bucket of Blood* abounded with beards, coffeehouses, and shabby clothes, not to mention abstract paintings and free verse, which made average Americans almost as suspicious as the Beats themselves did. Hollywood comedies like *Bell, Book, and Candle* featured Beat characters, and *Funny Face* paid an amusing visit to a cult of "Empathicalists," satirizing the beret-wearing existentialists who inspired some elements of Beat philosophy. Todd and Buzz, the peripatetic heroes of *Route 66,* traded the 1949 Hudson of *On the Road* for a 1960 Chevrolet Corvette as they tooled down the American highway in search of "a place where we really fit," as Buzz put it around the midpoint of this widely viewed CBS series. A year before its 1960 premiere, CBS's sitcom *The Many Loves of Dobie Gillis* brought beatnik Maynard G. Krebs to TV screens, yelping "Work?!!?" every time that four-letter word was spoken in his presence.

While these caricatures hardly elevated the Beats' public image, they were positively gentle compared with many treatments in the mainstream press. "The Only Rebellion Around," a widely read *Life* article, likened beatniks to hairy "fruit flies" infesting "the biggest, sweetest and most succulent casaba ever produced by the melon patch of civilization," this being the United States in 1959. The article ended with the question "a hundred million squares" must be asking themselves: "What have we done to deserve this?"

Ironically, even the most insulting portrayals increased the fame and media leverage of what was still a small, largely introverted group. Angry as they were at contemptuous accounts of their lives and works, the Beats were happy to sell books and disseminate ideas on the coattails of their newfound celebrity. Their days in the sun lasted about a dozen years, from the publication of *On the Road* until Kerouac's death in 1969, by which time the hippies were solidly ensconced as the American youth movement par excellence. During this period, serious-minded films about the Beat subculture offered some competition to their pop-movie counterparts. These included John Cassavetes's edgy *Shadows* and *The Connection* by Shirley Clarke, based on the Living Theatre's innovative New York production of Jack Gelber's groundbreaking play. Sundry avant-garde filmmakers also pursued Beat-related goals, from the Baudelairian hijinks of Ken Jacobs's *Little Stabs at Happiness* to the radical subjectivity of Stan Brakhage's eight-millimeter *Songs* and the hyperbolic surrealism and ferocious social commentary of Bruce Conner's frenetic found-footage collages. Not to mention *Pull My Daisy,* directed by photographer Robert Frank and painter Alfred Lesley, with such Beat icons as Ginsberg and Gregory Corso in the cast and narration improvised by Kerouac on the sound track.[1]

Throughout this time, the Beats worked hard to criticize the conformity and conservatism that they saw as spiritual toxins suffusing the postwar American dream. One of the Beat movement's most paradoxical qualities, however, is that it was never a movement at all, in the sense of a methodical effort to bring about fundamental sociopolitical change. Historical overviews are only half right when they imply clear connections between fractious Beat personalities and the waves of activism that gathered momentum in their wake. Agitators of the sixties and seventies often shared the Beats' rebellious spirit but not always their deeply felt sense that personal regeneration would bear far greater fruits than political struggle ever could. Beats certainly hoped their passionate rejection of consumerism and regimentation would inspire others to purge their lives and souls of spiritually deadening dross. But they called for the remaking of consciousness on a profoundly inward-looking basis, cultivating "the unspeakable visions of the individual," in Kerouac's resonant phrase. The idea was to revitalize society by revolutionizing thought, not the other way around. Kerouac confirmed this in 1968 when he told interviewer William F. Buckley Jr. that he repudiated words like *mutiny* and *insurrection,* standing for "order, tenderness, and piety" instead—none of which he would define in terms very much like Buckley's, needless to say.

The paradoxical patterns that arose within the Beat scene—aspirations toward aesthetic and spiritual purity on one hand, opportunities for social and cultural influence on the other—were never entirely resolved. This didn't faze them, since they were adept at writing off their inconsistencies as mind-expanding manifestations of bebop spontaneity, Zen-like transcendentalism, and plain old hipster smarts. In more recent years, the nebulous aspects of the Beat agenda help explain its appeal in the Reagan-Bush-Clinton-Bush era. From the punks to the slackers to Generation X, the very monikers of many youth-culture groups have reflected the Beat tradition of mixing antiauthoritarian exasperation with cynicism about clearly targeted protest. While these generations have lacked the profound Beat confidence in intuitive creativity and spiritual wisdom, they have been broadly in tune with their predecessors' distrustful stance toward top-down organization and conventional notions of propriety, decency, and decorum.

Popular accounts of the Beat sensibility often skim over the group's deepest ideals and highest aspirations, focusing more on the cultural novelty that made the Beat scene so transfixing for square outsiders. Such accounts also show scant interest in the diversity of the core Beat figures, who had so little in common (besides a fondness for spontaneous creativity) that Burroughs eventually declared they should not be called a group at all.

This casualness about artistic ambitions and personal relationships would have bothered Kerouac, who dubbed himself a "great rememberer redeeming life from darkness" and devoted his career to memorializing the impressions he had gathered while meandering down actual and imaginary roads. His emotionally pungent descriptions of people, places, and adventures have an extroverted quality that has served him well with readers for almost half a century. Yet writing was an intensely introspective process for him, blurring boundaries between reality and recollection, conscious and unconscious, physics and metaphysics. He was utterly serious about his "first thought best thought" credo—even criticizing Ginsberg for correcting typographical errors in his manuscripts—and he was equally passionate about the content of his books, down to the tiniest details.

The other key Beats pursued similar goals in different ways, violating every conventional rule they ran up against—Ginsberg with his endlessly eclectic poetry, Burroughs with his cut-up and folded-in prose—so as to extract unearthly truths that traditional techniques could never reach. There was something oddly cinematic in this effort to locate and explore a dimension that eludes ordinary kinds of perception. In a 1958 essay, Beat fellow traveler John Clellon Holmes imagined Kerouac in one of his trance-like writing sessions, "recording the 'movie' unreeling in his mind." Not surprisingly, all the leading Beats were movie fans, and each dreamed occasionally of making his own films, creating Hollywood magic that would somehow be unencumbered by Hollywood's money-minded motives. They shared a taste for Saturday-night entertainment, moreover: Kerouac saw Walt Disney's whimsy-filled *Fantasia* a whopping fifteen times, for instance, and Burroughs thought *The Wild Bunch* was terrific.

But what they dreamed most ardently of finding were what Kerouac called "eyeball kicks," the jolts of cosmic energy that separate everyday diversions from visionary art. Underpinning their willful eccentricities and merry pranks was a passionate search for unprecedented ways of living, communicating, thinking, and being. No film about them has evoked this as successfully as their own best verse and prose, although some that share their avant-garde radicalism have come impressively close.

The essays in this book are different in subject, approach, and tone, in the varied spirit of the diversified Beat writers themselves. The first, "Beats, Movies, and Ills of Postwar America," is the most sociologically oriented, tracing ways in which unconscionable streaks of racial and ethnic bias carved regressive scars into Beat writing and mainstream cinema alike—and reminding us that the Beats have lessons to convey to the twenty-first century in negative as well as positive terms. The second, "Lisped, Muxed, and Completely Flunk: Jack Kerouac Meets the Three Stooges," is what Kerouac might have called a "bookmovie" riff, set off in my mind by the energy of his great *Visions of Cody* and the looniness of the Three Stooges, whom Kerouac saw through an utterly original lens. The third, "*Desolation Angels:* Kerouac, Buddhism, and Film," explores in an intuitive way the sorts of multitudinous trails Kerouac's imagination took as he wrestled with literary and religious paradoxes that fascinated and bedeviled him throughout his career. The fourth, "Revision, Prevision, and the Aura of Improvisatory Art," is a more formal look at the notion of spontaneity as a recurring value in contemporary avant-garde culture. The fifth, "Constructing the Grotesque Body in Word, Image, and Sound," is another multimedia study, using a highly selective group of works to celebrate the merits of aesthetic freakishness—merits all of the core Beats recognized and emulated, each in his different and still-invigorating way.

ACKNOWLEDGMENTS

Many friends and colleagues provided witting and unwitting help during the years it took this volume to develop. So did my sons, Jeremy and Craig, with their unfailing intelligence and good humor. With regard to specific essays, I thank Bob Stam, Allen Weiss, and the late Walter Hitesman for ideas and inspiration that enriched my thinking about the concepts discussed in "Lisped, Muxed, and Completely Flunk: Jack Kerouac Meets the Three Stooges." A shorter version of that essay appeared in *Mosaic: A Journal for the Interdisciplinary Study of Literature* vol. 31, no. 4 (December 1998), pp. 83–98, as "Kerouac, Artaud, and the Baroque Period of the Three Stooges," and I thank *Mosaic* for permission to print the longer version here. I also thank the *Journal of Aesthetics and Art Criticism,* published by Blackwell Publishing Ltd., for permission to reprint "Revision, Prevision, and the Aura of Improvisatory Art," which appeared in vol. 58, no. 2 (spring 2000) in a slightly different form. I also acknowledge the helpfulness of comments about "*Desolation Angels:* Kerouac, Buddhism, and Film" I received at a conference of the Society for

Cinema Studies (now the Society for Cinema and Media Studies) in La Jolla, California, in March 1998, where I presented an earlier version entitled "Film, Buddhism, and the Beat Sensibility" in the "Buddhism and Cinema" panel chaired by David James.

Thanks go as well to the Research Committee of the C. W. Post Campus of Long Island University, which has generously provided me with research time that benefited this project a great deal.

Much gratitude is due to the Columbia University Seminar on Cinema and Interdisciplinary Interpretation, of which I have the honor to be cochair, for an incalculable amount of collegial support. Special thanks go to my cochair Bill Luhr, a close friend as well as a brilliant colleague, and to Krin Gabbard, Chris Sharrett, Pam Grace, Cindy Lucia, Sid Gottlieb, and others too numerous to mention. They know who they are.

Ray Carney has broadened my understanding of the Beats in many conversations over the years, and I have benefited as well from reading and knowing Regina Weinreich and Les Friedman, among others.

I also thank my excellent editors at Southern Illinois University Press: Karl Kageff, Wayne Larsen, and all who helped make this volume possible.

Last but the opposite of least is Mikita Brottman, who has helped me in an uncountable number of personal and professional ways. My gratitude is boundless.

Screening the Beats

BEATS, MOVIES, AND ILLS OF POSTWAR AMERICA

> Issues. Fuck Issues.
>
> —Jack Kerouac

The era commonly called the fifties began in the late 1940s, immediately after World War II, and persisted into the early sixties, when the rise of the hippies brought a set of radical new twists to American youth culture. The fifties were marked—scarred is a better word—by a remarkable number of qualities and imperatives beginning with the letter *c*. Consensus. Conformity. Conservatism. Consumerism. Common sense. Cold war.

To be sure, most middle-class Americans were at least peripherally aware that the values represented by hugely popular television programs like *The Adventures of Ozzie and Harriet* and *Leave It to Beaver* were preposterously sterile and simplistic; but those same Americans wanted to believe in them anyway. The reigning sociocultural creed assumed that, for most intents and purposes, an updated version of the old Victorian system remained expedient and efficient: Daddies make daily trips to the big city in quest of whatever money and power they can lay their hands on, mommies stay in the peaceful suburbs to tend the home and kids, and leisure days are togetherness times when everyone's labor pays off. Citizens who choose not to fit this pattern, or prove incapable of doing so, are eccentric, incompetent, or both. Evidence that large numbers of people were squeezed out of the system from the start—prevented from the option of fully participating by factors of race, class, gender, sexuality, and other contingencies eluding individual control—was ignored, denied, overlooked, and generally swept under the rug by every opinion-shaping force from the mass communications media to localized networks of education, religion, and gossip.

None of which meant that a debilitating web of social and cultural ills was not present, powerful, and pervasive. Sexism, ethnic and religious prejudice, homophobia—as yet unnamed—and other forms of bias suffused the status quo, confirming that the broad American consensus was built on a foundation much shakier than its public proponents would have had their readers, audiences, and students believe. Critics willing to open their eyes and minds perceived that American society was fraught with pernicious manifestations of inequity, bigotry, and socioeconomic malignancy. Nor were the critics themselves immune to such biases; analysts and arbiters sensitive to one facet of social dysfunction often remained blind to others. Even such a self-defined maverick as Beat author Jack Kerouac was a profoundly conservative thinker in many respects, notwithstanding his predilection for intoxicants and sexual adventures. As biographer Dennis McNally writes, "Racism and violence were not issues—'Issues,' he'd say with a curling sneer, 'Fuck issues'—but sins, and for that only penance was possible."[1] In this area, Kerouac took a position compatible with that of so-called Christian conservatives, including the recent breed of activists and acolytes who have flourished from the eighties through the present day, holding the moral category of sin to be more appropriate than the political category of social analysis when it comes to assessing and dealing with societal ills.

In short, cultural powers as different as the Hollywood film establishment and the Beat literary enclave fell prey to the influence of regrettable hegemonic assumptions and to the temptation (consciously recognized or not) to reproduce and reinforce them. I have chosen Hollywood cinema and Beat literature as gateways into the fifties social-power system because of their complementary qualities. Hollywood, newly challenged by television and shifting recreational patterns, was still in the last phase of the firmly established studio system that had shored up its economic and discursive vigor since the 1920s; it remained a potent source of social suasion, most of it dedicated to rationalizing and reconfirming a diffuse set of ingrained social and cultural assumptions. Beat writing, carefully read by relatively few but widely known via commentary and parody in the mass media, was regarded by sympathizers and detractors alike as a source of ornery, often flamboyant criticism of the so-called American dream. To underscore the blind spots of Hollywood film is to note how lacking in perceptivity the most powerful mass-audience medium in history was willing, perhaps eager, to be. To do the same with the Beat Generation writers is to highlight a similar lack of discernment in artists and communicators who presented themselves as the heralds and sages of a newly enlightened era freed from outmoded paradigms. To focus my argument, I will use the pervasiveness of racial and anti-Semitic bias as my frame of reference—not because these were the only major fault lines of the fifties but because they were among the most insidious and persistent.

Divided America

Socially, culturally, and economically, the United States was deeply divided along racial lines during the postwar era, as it had been—in different ways during different periods—throughout its history. As late as the early sixties, poll taxes and state-mandated literacy and intelligence tests (often rigged) prevented a large proportion of African Americans in the rural South from exercising their right to vote, and terrorist groups such as the Ku Klux Klan and the White Citizens Councils maintained a forceful reign of white supremacy.[2] Poverty among nonwhites was pervasive in its scope and often appalling in its severity.

Yet preoccupation with the cold war and the crusade against Communism served as both a reason and an excuse for conservatives, middle-of-the-roaders, and even most liberals of the period to engage in a policy of denial regarding such difficulties, not only insisting but apparently believing that the United States was becoming steadily more egalitarian in its prosperity.[3] Economic growth and managerial know-how were seen as the solutions to persistent inequality and dangers of class conflict, and such phenomena as "pockets of poverty" were looked upon as anomalies that would soon be eradicated.[4] Such cracks in the national facade were too deep to be completely obscured or obfuscated, however, and despite the majoritarian denial, they continued to make their presence felt in ways that eventually led to the outbreak of the civil-rights and social-freedom movements that played so great a role in politicizing the American mood (and American artists, including Beats like Allen Ginsberg and Beat-friendly filmmakers like Jonas Mekas) during the sixties.

Jews also felt uneasiness during the fifties, in part because of the lingering reality of American anti-Semitism and a growing body of knowledge about the Holocaust that had so recently taken place in European nations to which many American immigrants traced their roots. Muting the severity of Jewish anxiety, however, was the fact (reflected in surveys) that anti-Semitic feelings declined between the mid-forties and the mid-sixties.[5] This decline reflects the bad name, so to speak, that the still-fresh horrors of the Holocaust had given to anti-Semitism among Americans who had been inclined in that direction before the extent of Nazi evil was revealed. Excuses and rationalizations for anti-Jewish attitudes were also rendered newly problematic by the creation of the state of Israel and related sociopolitical developments.

Another reason for the reduction in anti-Semitism is that

generalized attitudes of all kinds toward Jews, both unfavorable and favorable, diminished during the postwar period. While this change may be taken as a positive development, reflecting a downturn in stereotyping, it may also be interpreted as a cautionary sign, indicating that Jews were being relegated to a more marginalized position in the national psyche.[6] Some commentators have claimed that Jews themselves helped bring about this decreased visibility by a defensive practice of attempting not to "stand out" in daily life—here one detects an ethnically tinged echo of the "averageness" sought by characters in such films as *The Man in the Gray Flannel Suit* (1956) and *In a Lonely Place* (1950)—and by cooperating with a tendency toward "de-Semitization" in the arts, whereby Jewish characters, names, and even the word *Jew* were avoided. "If we pretend that the Jew does not exist, the reasoning goes, then he will not be noticed," according to Henry Popkin's 1952 *Commentary* account of the rationale behind this practice; "the anti-Semite, unable to find his victim, will simply forget about him."[7] In the sociopolitical world, many Jews similarly aligned themselves with "universalistic" causes devoted to championing all minorities and fighting all social ills rather than singling out those with particular relevance to the Jewish community. Even such a seemingly constructive film as *The Diary of Anne Frank*, directed by George Stevens in 1959, has been cited as evidence of this trend, insofar as its portrait of Jewish suffering stands for suffering in general and warns against the woeful results of broadly based evils such as racism and betrayal; what critic Judith E. Doneson calls its "universalization and Americanization" suited the prevailing social mood of liberalism, consensus, and homogeneity.[8] In any case, the movement of many Jews toward Americanization did not persuade all Americans to abandon the anti-Jewish currents of the past, and horrifying incidents of overt, even violent hostility toward Jews remained far from unknown. The first two months of 1960, for instance, witnessed at least 643 incidents of desecration aimed at Jewish synagogues, cemeteries, stores, and homes.[9]

Looking at the causes, manifestations, and results of fifties-era biases, one observes many differences in the ways they affected African American and Jewish people. Still, the patterns of bigotry against these two groups made a peculiarly balanced pair in many respects, revealing distinct but related facets of a single malignant phenomenon. A study by Thomas F. Pettigrew, for instance, observed in 1966 that "Jews and others of immigrant stock have been traditionally criticized for failing to enter the mainstream of American culture; Negroes have been traditionally rebuked for wishing to enter it. Anti-Semitism is often most widespread among upper-status individuals; Negrophobia is frequently most common among persons of lower status."[10] Pettigrew's analysis suggests a sort of morbid symmetry in the paradigms of prejudice.

This idea gains support from the psychoanalytic view proposed by Bruno Bettelheim and Morris Janowitz, who reported in 1950 that intolerant people tend "to select the Jew for projecting onto him those tendencies rejected by the superego (for instance, the individual's desire to take advantage of others), while id desires were projected onto the Negro, whose supposed greater irrationality seemed to make him a suitable representative of the pressures originating in the irrational id."[11] Therefore the stereotypes applied most often to African Americans, "that they are dirty and that they depreciate property," are "related to id demands" and "contain symbols which are closely connected with anal preoccupation; the first directly, the second as the accusation that the Negro destroys what is the frequent, and in our society, the most highly esteemed reaction-formation against anality: wealth." Similarly, the stereotypes applied most often to Jews were "that they are clannish and help one another, and that they have the money. Helping one another is certainly a superego demand. . . . Interest in the possession of money—quite apart from the high status it provides in our society—is certainly a reaction-formation, developed under societal and superego pressure, against the primitive interest in dirt."[12] These stereotypes help explain the prevalence of such anti-Semitic labels as *ambitious, striving, crafty, clannish, shrewd, hyperintelligent, sly, dishonest;* and of such antiblack adjectives as *unambitious, lazy, happy-go-lucky, irresponsible, stupid, dirty, smelly, uninhibited, oversexed.* Since intergroup animosity is "a projection of the bigot's unacceptable inner impulses," in Pettigrew's words, the prejudiced person's own "superego sins . . . such as ambition, deceit and egotism" are personified in the stereotyped Jew while "id sins of the flesh" are perceived as characteristics of the stereotyped African American.[13]

Bigotry in Film

Antiblack and anti-Semitic attitudes, from the subtly patronizing to the outwardly antagonistic, found persistent echoes in American film and television of the fifties, usually in muted or disguised forms calculated to have a minimally adverse impact on movie ticket sales and the never-ending scramble for high TV ratings. Media executives sought to indulge the prejudices of their majority audiences while not foisting too much egregious offensiveness onto minority-group members—who were ticket buyers and TV watchers themselves—or onto majority-group members who might not like to think of themselves as prejudiced or mean-spirited even if they did accept demeaning images of minorities. Strategies of the studios and stations included clever marketing and reliance on the internalized acceptance (or at least tolerance) of stereotypes by subaltern as well as dominating groups.

A review of fifties-era cinema, and of film-historical writing on the period, finds ready evidence of such biased attitudes. One important survey, by African American film historian Donald Bogle, begins its account of the fifties by describing the decade as a turbulent time during which social and political changes wrought significant alterations within the film industry.[14] Bogle correctly notes the relatively individualistic mind-sets of independent producers and directors at this time, as compared with the mass-market mentality of most filmmakers who had flourished under the ironclad studio system of previous decades; and he notes other changes in the industry and its environment, such as the effect of TV competition on box-office figures. An important result of these phenomena is an interest in social-issue "problem pictures" and other films with comparatively serious concerns, which had become more numerous during the immediate postwar years. Socially substantial movies like these had enabled African American performers to make significant gains right after the war, and blacks were able to build on this during the fifties, which saw a further emergence of distinct and idiosyncratic African American screen personalities, protagonists, and themes.

Still and all, Bogle's subsequent analysis points up the gaping holes that overarching fifties values poked in these putative social-cinematic gains. He notes, for example, that the Fred Zinnemann–Stanley Kramer drama *The Member of the Wedding* (1952) marked the first time a black actress was allowed to dominate a major-studio white production, and that it launched Ethel Waters to stardom in the worlds of Hollywood film, Broadway theater, and network television. Yet he goes on to observe that her popularity faded in the mid-fifties, when her very individuality—unfashionable in an age that valued uniformity—made her appear a laudable but outmoded figure.[15] Dorothy Dandridge came into the fifties with intensity and individuality; yet her image was based on venerable tragic-mulatto clichés, and her career—which included such major films as *Carmen Jones* (1954) and *Porgy and Bess* (1959), both directed by the bold Otto Preminger—was sadly shadowed by a real-life drama in which racial biases rendered her trapped and unfulfilled. Sidney Poitier achieved great success partly because of his talents and partly because his acceptability to whites and blacks alike made him a model hero for integrationists. But it was also because he was not averse to playing "mild-mannered toms" in such pictures as *Edge of the City* (1957), where his character "falls into the tradition of the dying slave content that he has well served the massa," and *The Defiant Ones* (1959), where his self-sacrifice for a white man's sake drew jeers from inner-city audiences newly aware of "the great tomism inherent in the Poitier character, indeed in the Poitier image," as Bogle writes.

And so things went, notwithstanding happy exceptions along the way. Bogle finds the fifties film version of Richard Wright's novel *Native Son* (1951) an "ill conceived and technically poor . . . fiasco"; the baseball biopic *The Jackie Robinson Story* (1950) "lacked drama and direction"; singing star Harry Belafonte's screen career made moviegoers skeptically ask, "[I]f a black buck is not going to be daring or flashy or uninhibitedly sexy, then what good is he?" Putting as reputable a face as he can on black-related cinema of the fifties, Bogle still cannot avoid the fact that racial issues were treated with only "as much integrity as the film industry was capable of giving"; and on Bogle's own evidence, this was extremely limited. Movie after movie "failed to record black anger and anguish realistically," or "naively announced that integration would solve our problems," or "returned to idealized, fake black worlds." This is a sorry record even when considered in the overall sociopolitical context of the era.

Turning to the issue of Jewish subjects in Hollywood movies, the fifties were again less than distinguished. Film historian Lester Friedman overstates the period's blandness and timidity when he likens it to the thirties, a notoriously poor time for Jewish-American movies. Friedman is persuasive, however, when he argues that despite the proximity of the Holocaust and the new fascination with Israel, fifties Hollywood felt a sense of hesitancy regarding Jewish issues. This led studio filmmakers to avoid once-noteworthy issues such as Jewish-Gentile love and intermarriage, to overlook fresh issues such as the problems of Jews in changing urban areas, and to brush aside the special perspective of Jewish intellectuals, who were dismissed by Hollywood opinion makers as East Coast elitists.[16]

Supporting the view that Jewish distinctiveness was largely elided in fifties films, critic Patricia Erens divides pre-1958 dramas about Jews into two categories: those such as *The Caine*

Mutiny (1954) and *The Big Knife* (1955), in which ethnic elements play a minimal role, and those such as *The Magnificent Yankee* (1951) and *Good Morning, Miss Dove* (1955), in which the appearance of Jewish characters as outsiders allows other people to enlarge their moral horizons—pretty much the same function that the breezily observed African American community served for Kerouac during his *On the Road* years. Jewish comedy fell to new lows during the fifties, meanwhile, with few comic films containing recognizable Jewish characters of any kind. The years after 1957 did witness a flowering of movies on Jewish-American subjects, such as *Marjorie Morningstar* (1958) and *The Last Angry Man* (1959), largely written by Jews and reflecting a new interest among the general public in novels, plays, and films dealing with Jewish life. A cycle of films about Israel also emerged, beginning with *Sword in the Desert* (1949) and continuing in such movies as *The Juggler* (1953) and *Exodus* (1960). By contrast, however, film biographies tended to downplay or eliminate references to Jewish identity. At best, the fifties can be seen as a time of passage to a renewal of the Jewish image that would bear more fruit in the sixties.[17]

One helpful indicator of Hollywood's attitude toward Jews and Jewish culture is its treatment—or nontreatment—of the Holocaust, which was an immediate and overwhelming memory in the postwar decades. Judaic scholar Ilan Avisar argues that two moral and aesthetic dimensions are central to Holocaust films: that of representation, which is responsible for registering Nazi evil in all its horror, and that of presentation, which entails portraying and honoring the Jewish victims of Nazism without distortion.[18] In an analysis employing the concepts of universalization and marginalization that I have cited in somewhat different contexts above, Avisar concludes that Hollywood films have failed on both counts. The rhetoric of universalization aims at denying the singularity of the Holocaust by downplaying Jewish identity or having Jewish victims declare that people of all kinds must undergo suffering; designed to cushion film audiences from the discomfort of facing unspeakable realities, such rhetoric spins away from the fact that Nazi genocide was nourished by Christian bigotry and abetted by indifference from the civilized world at large. Eager to ease public guilt, Hollywood habitually presents Jews as not too different from the people who caused or tolerated their torment, suggesting that everybody is guilty, everybody suffers, redemption is still possible, and human beings are basically good.

The Diary of Anne Frank is an apt metaphor for dominant American attitudes toward Jews in the fifties. Doneson summarizes Anne's message as, "We are not the only ones to suffer . . . sometimes one race, sometimes another." In this way, Anne's suffering is made to symbolize suffering as a generalized occurrence. Via such universalizing strategies, the American imagination attempts to appropriate and Americanize the Holocaust and its memory—despite the facts that most Americans did not experience the Holocaust and that such appropriation minimizes its Jewish particularity.[19] The moral and ontological authenticity of such discourse is rendered even more spurious by the melodramatic nature of *The Diary of Anne Frank* and other films that solicit psychological gratification rather than ethical outrage from their spectators. *The Diary of Anne Frank* and Kramer's *Judgment at Nuremberg* (1961), about an American judge presiding over a Holocaust war-crimes trial, have been aptly cited by Holocaust-film scholar Annette Insdorf as productions that carve Holocaust material to fit the Procrustean bed of classical Hollywood style, thus comforting instead of confronting their spectators. (This danger is precisely what Bertolt Brecht sought to combat through his Epic theater, with its "alienation effect" and encouragement of cognitive response from the audience, rather than merely emotional or psychological response.) By contrast with those movies, Preminger's *Exodus* takes the more thoughtful course of evoking Holocaust extermination through a verbal account that bypasses Hollywood's usual brand of wordy histrionics.[20]

American attitudes toward Jews during the postwar period may also be assessed through films not specifically related to Holocaust themes. Two films on anti-Semitism in American life, Edward Dmytryk's *Crossfire* and Elia Kazan's *Gentleman's Agreement,* were released soon after the war in 1947, and both have been criticized within the Jewish community as inadequate to the profundity and complexity of their subject. *Crossfire,* which has been cited as the first American film explicitly addressing American anti-Semitism, is a film-noir suspense drama about the effort of a police inspector (Robert Young) to identify and apprehend a psychopathic former soldier (Robert Ryan) who has murdered a Jewish man (Sam Levene). One of the dialogue exchanges meant to reveal the villain's anti-Semitism takes place when he is being questioned by the police officer. "I've seen a lot of guys like him," says the still-unidentified killer of the Jewish victim, whom he had met in a bar on the night of the murder. "Guys that played it safe during the war . . . keeping themselves in civvies and a swell apartment. . . ." Spectators of the film are not supposed to like this character or approve of his words. Yet commentator E. E. Cohen noted in 1947 that the film itself constructs the victim-character as "a composite of many of the anti-Semitic stereotypes of the Jew—soft-handed, flashily dressed, suave, artistic, intellectual, moralizing, comfortably berthed in a cushy bachelor apartment during a war, with a bosomy Gentile mistress, self-assured, pushing in where he is not wanted."[21] Also significant is the film's assumption that while anti-Semitism may have diversified outlets, it can be likened to a bedrock emotion carried within an afflicted individual, oblivious to social and cultural surroundings, ready to explode when provoked by an appropriate stimulus. Says the police-officer hero about Monty, the killer,

> This, um, business of hating Jews comes in a lot of different sizes. There's the, uh, you-can't-join-our-country-club kind; the you-can't-live-around-here kind; yes, and

> the you-can't-work-here kind. And because we stand for all of these, we get Monty's kind. He's just one guy, we don't get him very often, but he grows out of all the rest. . . . You know we have a law against carrying a gun? Well, we have that law because a gun is dangerous. Well, hate—Monty's kind of hate—is like a gun. If you carry it around with you it can go off and kill somebody. It killed Samuels last night.

Gentleman's Agreement stars Gregory Peck as a journalist who poses as a Jew in order to have the "experience" of anti-Semitism so he can write critically about it. Although the film means well, it makes enough missteps to render its message less than effective. One of the most glaring takes place when the hero's young son tearfully complains that other children have tormented him for being Jewish—whereupon a helpful adult tries to comfort him not by attacking the fatuity of anti-Semitism but by assuring him that he is not really Jewish. Also of interest is the fact that the film's Gentile characters appear to have little or no connection with religions of their own; the Peck character must patiently explain the meaning of churchgoing to his son, who has evidently had no contact with it. The subtle message embedded in Moss Hart's screenplay is that Gentiles have less need than Jews for religious identity and tradition.[22]

No further Hollywood films were made about problems of anti-Semitism for some years, compounding the impression that the attitude of Hollywood and Hollywood's audience toward Jews was less sophisticated at best, and less decent at worst, than a morally sensitive observer would have wished. War movies did flourish during the fifties, and in the wake of World War II and the Holocaust, one might have hoped they would give prominent attention to the anguish of recent Jewish history. Regrettably, however, fifties war films followed a prevailing tendency of the cold-war period (when anxiety over Communism overshadowed the memory of past traumas) by showing the German people as downtrodden losers deserving of generalized compassion for their own World War II travails.[23] The most positive thing to be said about Hollywood in this context is that not all its productions followed simplistic patterns. An example of a more sophisticated work—which nonetheless adheres closely to audience-friendly formulas—is Douglas Sirk's melodrama *A Time to Love and a Time to Die* (1958), based on the novel by Erich Maria Remarque, who plays a small role in the movie. It stars John Gavin as a German soldier suffering a profound moral dilemma that stems less from romantic and family problems than from his loss of all belief in the cause for which he, his army, and his country are fighting. The spectacle of a young man trudging back into combat while desperately hoping his side will lose is eminently Sirkian, and indicates that Hollywood was not entirely bereft of ethically redeeming projects, however intermittently they may have arisen.

Bias and the Beats

The writers of the Beat Generation entered the problem-ridden terrain of postwar America as rebels and reformers. Various biographers have confirmed this in accounts of individual Beat figures. Burroughs considered himself "the Great Seceder, the artist as outlaw," writes Ted Morgan, with an "antipathy for all forms of control."[24] Kerouac was "obsessed, enraged, with a sense of America being debauched by the clanking, alienating horror called the new industrial state," in Dennis McNally's words.[25] Ginsberg felt the problems of the world were "conceptual, the result of the [national] powers attempting to force a single consciousness on the masses," reports Michael Schumacher, whose critical reference to "a single consciousness" recalls Soviet literary theorist Mikhail Bakhtin's preference for the boisterousness and multiplicity of "dialogic" art over the uniformity and homogeneity of "monologic" expression.[26]

One might have expected unconventional thinkers like the Beats to see through and take up arms against the oppressive forces at work within the social-political and cultural-aesthetic arenas of their day. Yet notwithstanding their oppositional stances toward official thought, these putative nonconformists hardly escaped the monologizing tendencies of the sociocultural ethos surrounding them. This is evident in attitudes harbored by the Beats themselves toward subaltern racial and religious groups.

With regard to anti-Semitic feelings, Kerouac appears to have been the most susceptible. When his friends Ginsberg and Carl Solomon criticized the content and accessibility of his novels *On the Road* and *Doctor Sax: Faust Part Three* in 1952, he saw himself (according to Gerald Nicosia's biography) as "a peasant, a Lil Abner among slick, pitiless Jewish businessmen," and he relived memories of being humiliated by "the millionaire Jews of Horace Mann" during his prep-school days.[27] Writing of the Horace Mann School in one of his most important late novels, *Vanity of Duluoz: An Adventurous Education, 1935–46,* he refers to two schoolmates as "Germans who came from rich families (not Jews but real Germans)"[28]—a phrase that unwittingly mirrors the ethnic slur ("Marx wasn't German, he was a Jew") that exposes the character played by Orson Welles in *The Stranger* (1946) as a Nazi villain. (*The Stranger* was also directed by Welles, incidentally, a filmmaker Kerouac much admired.) By the beginning of the sixties, Kerouac had unloaded years of anti-Semitic epithets on Ginsberg, who had decided to disregard such insults rather than forfeit their longtime friendship.[29] Watching an old movie about Adolf Hitler on television in early 1961, with Kerouac and his notoriously bigoted mother, Ginsberg heard Kerouac agree with his mother's criticism of Jews for still complaining about the Holocaust and concur with her suggestion (aimed in Ginsberg's direction) that Hitler should have finished what he started.[30] The best that can be said for Kerouac is that his anti-Semitism appears to have been sporadic and inconsistent, and that he occasionally became disgusted with it himself—as in the mid-fifties, when he mixed self-reprobation *and* bigotry in a letter to a friend, writing, "That's the end when I start picking on poor dumb Jews."[31]

Burroughs denied harboring any anti-Semitic feelings, and when his confidante Brion Gysin objected to certain phrases in his novel *Cities of the Red Night* on the ground that they smacked of anti-Semitism, he asserted that his "Jew jokes" were justified since they were the expressions not of himself but of his characters. At the same time, however, he provided his associate with a brief catalogue of invective toward Jews in his earlier work: "*Naked Lunch:* 'All a Jew wants to do is diddle a Christian girl.' *Nova Express:* 'Take your ovens with you and pay Hitler on the way out. Nearly got the place hot enough for you Jews, didn't he?' *Exterminator!:* 'And I want to say this to followers of the Jewish religion. We like nice Jews with Jew jokes so watch yourself Jewboy or we'll cut the rest of it off.'"[32]

Ginsberg was Jewish but was also capable of making statements on subjects related to Jews and Judaism that seemed provocative to some and exasperating to others, as when he remarked of Israel in the early sixties that "[t]he trouble with the Israelis is that they are Jewish, they were hypnotized by the Nazis and all other racist magic hypnotists of previous eras. Astonishing mirror image resemblance between Nazi theory of racial superiority and Jewish hang-up as chosen race. They didn't desire it—any of them. Any fixed static categorized image of the Self is a big goof."[33]

The position of the Beats with regard to African American issues is more complex. Little in the way of conventional antiblack prejudice is reflected in their literary works, and Burroughs has been applauded as one of the rare American writers to be concerned with racism in the postwar years, perhaps because his roots in St. Louis on the Mississippi River gave him an understanding of the South that his colleagues did not share. Barry Miles gives an exaggerated impression of Burroughs's interest in conventional social protest when he suggests that expressions of outrage at the treatment of Southern blacks make *Naked Lunch* a precursor of the sixties civil-rights movement. Still, he is correct to cite that novel's recurring images of a burning black person and a "frog-faced fat Southern sheriff" as instances of corrosive criticism aimed directly at racial bigotry.[34]

By contrast, Ginsberg generally overlooks African American oppression as a concentrated locus of American injustice. Kerouac falls between him and Burroughs, expressing a romanticized view of African American life and experience that manifests *(a)* a healthy amount of admiration for black culture, history, and aesthetic expression and *(b)* an unfortunate amount of vicarious adventurism and naive primitivism or exoticism, with apparent motives ranging from the wistfully idealistic to the thoughtlessly parasitic. His last completed novel, *Pic,* is a sort of preteen *On the Road,* telling a comparatively conventional story of travel from North Carolina to New York City through the eyes (and dialect) of a black ten-year-old boy; although it incorporates many of the racial and regional clichés of its day, it shows respect as well as sympathy for its hero and his African American relatives and friends. Another side of Kerouac's racial consciousness is revealed in *On the Road* itself, which contains the most vivid instance of his naïveté with regard to postwar black America and to nonwhite America in general:

> At lilac evening I walked with every muscle aching among the lights of 27th and Welton in the Denver colored section, wishing I were a Negro, feeling that the best the white world had offered was not enough ecstasy for me, not enough life, joy, kicks, darkness, music, not enough night. . . . I wished I were a Denver Mexican, or even a poor overworked Jap, anything but what I was so drearily, a "white man" disillusioned. . . . I passed the dark porches of Mexican and Negro homes; soft voices were there, occasionally the dusky knee of some mysterious sensual gal; and dark faces of the men behind rose arbors. Little children sat like sages in ancient rocking chairs. . . . I was only myself, Sal Paradise, sad, strolling in this violet dark, this unbearably sweet night, wishing I could ex-

> change worlds with the happy, true-hearted, ecstatic Negroes of America.[35]

In outline, this is a vision worthy of simplistic scenes in the Walt Disney studio's *Song of the South* (1946), not to mention King Vidor's *Hallelujah* (1929) and other such antecedents. Kerouac seems unaware or unconcerned that the happiness, true-heartedness, and ecstasy of his heroes were often interfered with by the hates, fears, and violence of white people whose disillusionment took less poetic forms than his own. Interestingly, a National Film Board of Canada documentary, called *Jack Kerouac's Road: A Franco-American Odyssey* (1989), contains a passage in which this section of *On the Road* is quoted extensively on the sound track while images of African American life appear on the screen, and the latter do an efficient job of contradicting the romantic excesses of Kerouac's prose. Unfortunately, the overall tone of the documentary's near-hagiographic look at Kerouac indicates that the filmmakers sought only to illustrate the quoted material with superficially relevant images, and that the telling contradiction between the verbal and visual elements is unintentional.

The Subterraneans Versus MGM

The social, cultural, and political shortcomings of America in the fifties are (like those of America today) so sweeping, pervasive, and complex that no limited outline can do more than suggest their nature and seriousness, and emphasize the enormous gap that existed between the inescapable realities and frequently deluded self-perceptions of the era. The point of my brief survey is to underscore the remarkable amount of overlap among *(a)* the eagerness of Americans to embrace patently blinkered clichés about the essential rightness and soundness of the society in which they lived and worked, *(b)* the readiness of powerful media forces to reinforce and reproduce those clichés through the influential discourses of feature filmmaking, and *(c)* the willingness of so-called revolutionaries like the Beat writers to buy into strikingly similar ways of looking at and interacting with the cultural-political scene around them. I argue elsewhere in this volume that while bourgeois conformity and Beat rebellion represent fundamentally different responses to dominant ideological claims of the postwar period, they have more in common than vested interests of either stamp have ever felt comfortable with acknowledging. The sad parallels between, say, the essentialist account of anti-Semitism in *Crossfire* and Kerouac's crude remarks about Jewish businessmen reveal an indelible streak of all-American xenophobia that passes too easily across the allegedly great divide between self-satisfied average citizens and self-designated mavericks who present their insights as visionary critiques of all the traps into which their compatriots have fallen.

I will conclude with a final example taken from Kerouac's novel *The Subterraneans* and its Hollywood adaptation. The novel chronicles the love affair between Leo Percepied, one of Kerouac's virtually undisguised surrogates, and Mardou Fox, the pseudonym Kerouac gave to a real-life woman with whom he was emotionally and sexually involved. Kerouac-Percepied describes her background in both racial and sociocultural terms: "Negro mother dead for birth of her—unknown Cherokee-halfbreed father a hobo who'd come throwing torn shoes across gray plains of fall in black sombrero and pink scarf squatting by hotdog fires casting Tokay empties into the night 'Yaa Calexico!'"[36] The first impression she makes on the narrator derives much of its impact from the polysemic nuances he detects in her manner of speech: "my heart didn't exactly sink but wondered when I heard the cultured funny tones of part Beach, part I. Magnin model, part Berkeley, part Negro highclass, something, a mixture of *langue* and style of talking and use of words I'd never heard before except in certain rare girls of course *white* and so strange . . . definitely the new bop generation way of speaking. . . ."[37] In the real-world experience that inspired the novel, Kerouac's infatuation with her appears to have been inspired by deep and genuine affection; yet his eventual determination to end the relationship was accompanied by a feeling that she posed a long-term threat to what he called his "white man's life."[38] As recounted in the novel, moreover, even the passionate early stages of their relationship were hardly free from Kerouac's complicatedly racist feelings, which he reveals with frankness and embarrassment: for example, "so in the morning I wake from the scream of beermares and see beside me the Negro woman with parted lips sleeping, and little bits of white pillow stuffing in her black hair, feel almost revulsion, realize what a beast I am for feeling anything near it. . . ."[39]

Revealing a less self-critical brand of racism, Hollywood's 1960 adaptation of *The Subterraneans*—the only film version of a Beat novel made during the Beat period—transforms the black Mardou into a white Frenchwoman played by Leslie Caron, a bona fide star with such major pictures as Vincente Minnelli's *An American in Paris* (1951) and *Gigi* (1959) among her credits.[40] White though she may be, the film's Mardou is given a history of suffering worthy of her black prototype in the novel: "They drove my mother out of town . . . yelling and tearing at her," she declares on a poster for the movie. The willingness of the filmmakers to erase blackness and its history, in favor of a compulsory movie-whiteness as trite as it is predictable, is typical of Hollywood's mostly regrettable history with regard to racial prejudice. It would be heartening if one could say that Kerouac's novel represents a diametrically different perspective on such matters. But for all his romanticism about the life, joy, kicks, darkness, and music of black America, he found his "white man's life" too appealing to be easily relinquished or even seriously put at risk. At least he saw through his hypocrisy with enough clarity and candor to feel like a beast about it. It is hard to imagine the MGM production office falling prey to the same misgivings.

LISPED, MUXED, AND COMPLETELY FLUNK: JACK KEROUAC MEETS THE THREE STOOGES

> My rosy tomatoes
> pop squirting
> from your awful
> rotten grave—
>
> Your profile,
> erstwhile
> Garboesque,
> mistook by earth—
> eels for some
> fjord to
> Sheol—
>
> —Jack Kerouac, "A Curse at the Devil"

American life in the fifties was famously marked by conservative discourses, which were challenged (with varying degrees of sincerity and effectiveness) by a variety of questioning, hostile, and downright negational counterparts—or contravisions, to borrow a term from Stan Brakhage, perhaps the most radical avant-garde filmmaker to emerge during the period.[1] Such oppositional currents ranged from the socially skeptical scholarship of Paul Goodman and David Riesman to the far-reaching artistic explorations of Bud Powell and Miles Davis in music, Jackson Pollock and the New York School in painting, Edward Albee and the Living Theatre on the stage, and Kenneth Anger and Gregory J. Markopoulos in film, among others in sundry fields.[2]

Central to this activity was the literature of the Beat Generation writers. Allen Ginsberg's jazzlike poetry, William S. Burroughs's cut-up texts, and Jack Kerouac's peripatetic novels fell prey to social and political failings of their own. Yet these outpourings of spontaneous creativity were at once expressions of assertively "individualistic" personalities, explorations of fecund yet officially disregarded aesthetic possibilities, and deliberately chosen sociolinguistic responses to the homogenized tone of "authoritative" literature sanctioned by the academy, the bestseller list, or both.

To be sure, the Beats were not organized guerrillas recruiting partisans for group assaults on square ideology. Their rebellion took place on the dispersed terrain of scattered individual consciousness, not so much confronting the centers of organized power as ignoring or evading them. Yet this insurrection was no less carefully conceived or passionately pursued for being carried out through a combination of personal adventurism, aesthetic experimentalism, and intellectual eccentricity. It chipped away at dehumanizing norms by interrogating, demystifying, and ridiculing them, anchoring its own key values in the very oddness and unconventionality that rendered the Beats suspect in the eyes of the American mainstream.

In this essay, I will use Mikhail Bakhtin's theory of carnivalism to explore Kerouac's critique of postwar society, emphasizing such key Beat strategies as ambivalent rhetorical tropes and transgressive grotesque-body imagery. I will then suggest ways in which Kerouac's jazzlike riffs on such seemingly whimsical subjects as a movie actress's photo, an old folk song, and Hollywood slapstick fantasy share revealing characteristics with the similarly radical assault on twentieth-century sociocultural norms by playwright and culture theorist Antonin Artaud.

The Carnival Spirit

Kerouac thought of his work as "spontaneous bop prosody" and used his writing to rediscover in words, memories, and ideas an array of hidden or overlooked contextual meanings buried in the layers of his own consciousness and in the cultural forces surrounding him. This spontaneity and rediscovery are especially clear in such early works as *Doctor Sax: Faust Part Three* (1959) and *Visions of Cody* (published in 1972 but written twenty years earlier), two of Kerouac's most complex achievements. The allusiveness, polysemy, and slippage of conventional rationality that characterize these novels bear out the opposition of Beat writing to the unity and authority of most mainstream expression in the fifties period. From a Bakhtinian perspective, the books are rooted in the carnivalesque tradition that has mounted a centuries-long challenge to entrenched notions of social hierarchy, constructing extravagant visions of "life drawn out of its *usual* rut" and of "'life turned inside out,' 'the reverse side of the world' *('monde à l'envers')*."[3]

The carnival spirit has special importance in times of strong normative pressure. Pointing to the medieval period in Europe as such an era, Bakhtin notes that a typical person of that time lived two parallel lives. One was the "*official*" life, "subjugated to a strict hierarchical order, full of terror, dogmatism, reverence, and piety." Opposed to this was the life of carnival and the public square, "free and unrestricted, full of ambivalent laughter, blasphemy, the profanation of everything sacred . . . familiar contact with everyone and everything."[4]

Bakhtin's analysis may be applied mutatis mutandis to the period after World War II, when mainstream American culture attempted to nourish only the first of these two "lives," supporting it with claims of political and social-scientific veracity while discouraging tendencies toward "free and unrestricted" existence, that is, modes of living we might call *pararational,* since they hover between the strictures of socially accepted rationality and the unlimited *ir*rationality associated with radically altered states of consciousness such as psychosis and dementia.

Dominant discourses did not eradicate the carnivalistic sensibility, of course, but they did manage to divide the two kinds of "lives" between two highly asymmetrical groups. Proper middle-class citizens lived out something like the "official" life of the medieval subject—trudging through a round of socially sanctified activities, filling strictly designated niches in home and workplace, undergoing the terrors of cold-war paranoia while internalizing the dogmas of a culture obsessed with normality and averageness. It was left for the Beats and other self-styled rebels to live—or try to live—a more carnivalesque existence. One of their strategies was to nurture what Bakhtin calls the "image of the contradictory, perpetually becoming and unfinished being" within individual consciousness.[5] *Doctor Sax* and *Visions of Cody* provide vivid evidence as to how free of restriction, how blasphemous and profane, how charged with impudent ambivalence, how fruitfully familiar and radically vulgar the young Kerouac wanted his daily life, and the daily lives of everyone with whom he came into contact, to be.

To make this argument is not, of course, to posit rigid or impermeable distinctions between a straitjacketed bourgeoisie, on one hand, and an anything-goes bohemia, on the other, glaring at each other across some unbreachable boundary running from the reverentially hushed churches of the former to the wild-and-woolly coffeehouses of the latter. Respectable citizens of the Eisenhower age seized numerous opportunities for carnivalesque laughter and glancing contact with the subversive and profane; looking just at popular culture, examples range from Frank Tashlin's ribald movies and Ernie Kovacs's surreal TV shows to the drugged-up inflections of Jack Gelber's plays and the burgeoning bebop scene. Conversely, many a Beat renegade experienced moments of uncertainty, submissiveness, dogmatism, and even out-and-out traditionalism. Tracing his personal definition of the term *Beat* to the fulfillments offered by *beatitude,* Kerouac scorned sensationalistic phrases like "Beat mutiny" and "Beat insurrection," which were repeated ad nauseam in media accounts. "Being a Catholic," he told conservative journalist William F. Buckley Jr. in a late-sixties television appearance, "I believe in order, tenderness, and piety." In sum, while middle-class conformity and Beat contentiousness reflected radically different perspectives on the human condition, they were less sharply divided than ideologues on either side liked to imply.

Oscillation and Ambivalence

Kerouac's ability to scamper nimbly along this cultural continuum, embracing insights that less flexible minds would call contradictory, is echoed by what critic Regina Weinreich calls an "oscillating linguistic design" in his most important novels. This design asserts itself in rhetorical tensions such as dream versus Reality, comedy versus tragedy, racing up versus racing down, raging action versus gentle sweetness—and, more sweepingly, Lost Bliss versus Bliss Achieved, arching through entire novels and groups of novels.[6]

Kerouac's predilection for mutually contesting tropes plunges his work into the "ambivalence" that Bakhtin finds at the heart of carnivalism, where it characterizes phenomena ranging from the crowning and decrowning of a carnivalized authority figure—considered the "primary carnivalistic act" in Bakhtin's theory—to "the image of *fire* in carnival . . . that simultaneously destroys and renews the world." Also ambivalent are the combination of ridicule and rejoicing found in ritual laughter, and the deployment of parody as a sort of "system of crooked mirrors, elongating, diminishing, distorting in various directions and to various degrees" everything they reflect.[7] Such ambivalence is related to parody and to practices of literary doubling; this relationship is especially strong when doubling goes beyond the neat binarism of opposed essences and expresses the boisterous multiplicity of dialogic dissemination, bringing together such polar distinctions as "birth and death (the image of pregnant death), blessing and curse (benedictory carnival curses which call simultaneously for death and rebirth), praise and abuse, youth and old age, top and bottom, face and backside, stupidity and wisdom." Also typical of carnival thinking are "paired images, chosen for their contrast (high/low, fat/thin, etc.) or for their similarity (doubles/twins)."[8]

Kerouac's work is filled with doubles, in both its rhetorical oscillations and its narrative moments. One immediately thinks of the many masks and disguises he wears as the thinly veiled protagonist (Jack Duluoz, Sal Paradise, Leo Percepied, Ray Smith) of his various autobiographical novels. One also thinks of the resonant word and image conjunctions that he uses to carnivalize "proper" novelistic discourse. An early passage in *Doctor Sax,* for instance, referring to "the early Catholic childhood of Centralville," describes a characteristic vision: "Figures of coffinbearers emerging from a house on a rainy night bearing a box with dead old Mr. Yipe inside. The statue of Ste. Thérèse turning her head in an antique Catholic twenties film with Ste. Thérèse dashing across town in a car with W. C. Fieldsian close shaves by the young religious hero while the doll (not Ste. Thérèse herself but the lady hero symbolic thereof) heads for her saintliness with wide eyes of disbelief."[9] The discursive collisions in these two sentences are amazingly audacious, as the faceless Mr. Yipe compels the attention of a saint being chauffeured by a hero resembling not only W. C. Fields but also Kerouac's father, whom Kerouac likened to Fields more than once in his work. The multiple meanings here indicate Kerouac's carnivalistic willingness to group contrasting thoughts, feelings, facts, and personas into Rabelaisian concatenations that bring together "what had been hierarchically disunified and distant." Bakhtin cites this technique, along with a complementary "disunification of what had been traditionally linked," as a potent means of "serving to bring about . . . the materialization of the world."[10] Kerouac's enjoyment of combined oppositions—coffin bearers and dashing heroes, moribund corpses and speeding cars, religious icons and movie comedians, etc., etc.—expresses the rebellious mischievousness that is one of his most conspicuous literary traits.

One may say of his creative linkages what Bakhtin said of comparable inventions in François Rabelais's prose: that they aim "at destroying the established hierarchy of values, at bringing down the high and raising up the low, at destroying every nook and cranny of the habitual picture of the world."[11]

Kerouac frequently accomplishes these aims through an emphasis on physicality that has (at least by fifties standards) a decidedly Rabelaisian ring. Like his sixteenth-century predecessor as described by Bakhtin, he often seeks an expansively comic tonality that "not only destroys traditional connections and abolishes idealized strata [but] also brings out the crude, unmediated connections between things that people otherwise wish to keep separate, in pharisaical error." By doing this, he wishes "to demonstrate the whole remarkable complexity and depth of the human body and its life, to uncover a new meaning, a new place for human corporeality in the real spatial-temporal world," as Bakhtin expresses it, thus allowing the world itself to take on "new meaning and concrete reality, a new materiality" and to enter "a contact with human beings that is no longer symbolic but material."[12]

Kerouac's approach to materialized awareness is itself a deeply ambivalent enterprise, however, since yet another pairing in his life and work—an affinity with both Christian and Buddhist philosophy—leads him to complex religious inclinations that oscillate among affirmations of the flesh, of the spirit, and of flesh *and* spirit as commingled in the Roman Catholic theology (with its doctrines of incarnation and transubstantiation) that always played a part in his thinking. One imposing piece of evidence for his materiality-spirituality ambivalence is found at the end of *Vanity of Duluoz: An Adventurous Education, 1935–46,* which culminates the Duluoz Legend cycle comprising all of Kerouac's autobiographical novels.[13] The penultimate chapters of this book contain anguished broodings by alcohol-wracked Kerouac-Duluoz on several related issues; these include "the cruel nature of bestial creation . . . a mean heartless creation emanated by a God of Wrath, Jehovah, Yaweh, No-Name," and his dying father's "foolishness in ever believing that 'life' was worth anything but what it smells like down in the Bellevue Morgue."[14] He then berates both Jesus and Buddha for failing to explain how spiritual redemption can be possible "when you have to pass food in and out of your body's bag day in day out, how can you be 'saved' in a situation so sottish and flesh-hagged as that?" This last question leads to a vivid image of Buddha mouthing platitudes as he dies "at the age of eighty-three . . . in an awful pool of dysentery," and to a despairing observation that "[b]irth is the direct cause of all pain and death. . . . Spring is the laugh of a maniac, I say."

Here the intertwined phenomena of birth, death, and laughter are cast into a harsh perspective that smacks more of nightmare than of carnival. The tone undergoes an instantaneous transformation, however, when the narrator reports a vision of the cross, "just then when I closed my eyes after writing all this. I cant escape its mysterious penetration into all this brutality. . . . Madmen and suicidists see this. Also dying people and people in unbearable anguish." After returning to and wrapping up the narrative substance of the novel, he reaffirms his decision to complete the volume: "When this book is finished, which is going to be the sum and substance and crap of everything I've been thru throughout this whole gaddam life, I shall be redeemed." He then reports the mixed results of this venture ("I did it all . . . nothing ever came of it") and finally states,

> No "generation" is "new." There's "nothing new under the sun." "All is vanity."
>
> . . .
>
> Forget it, wifey. Go to sleep. Tomorrow's another day.

Hic calix!

Look that up in Latin, it means "Here's the chalice," and be sure there's wine in it.[15]

In the juxtaposition of statements and tonalities within this concluding moment, critic Gregory Stephenson finds an assertion that although our earthly endeavors are ultimately futile, ending in death and dust, we must believe that our actions have meaning and will somehow be redeemed in eternity. Similarly, the book's final imagery of chalice and wine refers both to Jesus's sacrifice for the sake of humanity and, more playfully, to the joys of life as represented by the recreation and release that Kerouac found in alcohol.[16] Drinking took a prodigious toll on him, with torturous effects that his novel *Big Sur* describes most harrowingly; yet it also provided him with such solace that he called alcoholism "the joyous disease." Ambivalent to the core, Kerouac maintained a profound investment in the very world that he sought through alcohol consumption to escape and through spiritual disciplines to transcend. In his writing and in his life, he never lost an ultimately mystical fascination with what critic John Tytell describes as "the bared power of the actual and the ordinary, the natural and the commonplace—like the road that became his primal metaphor."[17]

Pregnant Death

> Artistic morality, that was the point, because then I devised the idea of burning most of what I wrote so that my art would not appear (to myself as well as to others) to be done for ulterior, or practical motives, but just as a function, a daily duty, a daily scatalogical "heap" for the sake of purgation.
>
> —Kerouac, *Vanity of Duluoz*

> . . . a combination of nausea and the stirrings of the urino-genital tract.
>
> —*National Review* on Beat poetry, 1961

> Of course writing was the medium for this flooding soul semen of his. . . .
>
> —Seymour Krim, "Kerouac Dies for Me in Spain, with Wreath by Aronowitz"

The actual and the ordinary often mean the bodily for Kerouac, who peppers his 1958 article "Essentials of Spontaneous Prose" with a noteworthy number of somatic references. In punctuation, he likens the "vigorous space dash" to "jazz musician drawing breath between outblown phrases." In composition, he recommends not "pause to think of proper word" but rather "the infantile pileup of scatological buildup words till satisfaction is gained." In rhythm, he recommends working "excitedly, swiftly, with writing-or-typing-cramps, in accordance (as from center to periphery) with laws of orgasm, Reich's 'beclouding of consciousness.' *Come* from within, out—to relaxed and said."[18]

Kerouac draws on the oral, anal, and genital levels of writing activity not merely to offer a string of suggestive metaphors but to invoke verbal creation as an act of physical exchange and interpenetration with the world outside the self. In this way, Kerouac aligns himself with the carnivalesque tradition of discourse about the "grotesque body" and the "material bodily lower stratum," which Bakhtin exhaustively studied and continually celebrated. The grotesque image is, for Bakhtin, that which "reflects a phenomenon in transformation, an as yet unfinished metamorphosis, of death and birth, growth and becoming." His favored example is a group of figurines (in the Kerch terra-cotta collection) representing senile, pregnant, laughing hags who embody "a pregnant death, a death that gives birth." The grotesque body

> is not separated from the rest of the world. It is not a closed, completed unit; it is unfinished, outgrows itself, transgresses its own limits. The stress is laid on those parts of the body that are open to the outside world, that is, the parts through which the world enters the body or

> emerges from it, or through which the body itself goes out to meet the world. This means that the emphasis is on the apertures or the convexities, or on various ramifications and offshoots: the open mouth, the genital organs, the breasts, the phallus, the potbelly, the nose.[19]

Kerouac would surely have approved this enumeration. Mouths, genitals, and breasts recur with generous regularity in his prose adventures, as do other body parts. It is not mere coincidence, for example, that the Hollywood figure with whom he most repeatedly conflates his father's image is W. C. Fields, known throughout his film career for the proud potbelly and glowing nose that accompanied his drawling, insinuating voice. Kerouac was also familiar with intimations of life, pregnancy, and death as aspects of a single grotesque (and sometimes terrifying) cycle—as when he refers in *Vanity of Duluoz* to "Mother Kali of ancient India and its wisdom aeons with all her arms bejeweled, legs and belly too, gyrating insanely to eat back thru the only part of her that's not jeweled, her yoni, or yin, everything she's given birth to. Ha ha ha ha she's laughing as she dances on the dead she gave birth to. Mother Nature giving you birth and eating you back."[20] The spirit of Bakhtin's beloved figurines is clearly recognizable in this visionary incarnation of the grotesque-body tradition.

In general, Kerouac leans toward orality as the privileged site of interaction between self and world. He refers often to food, eating, and drinking as well as talking, conversing, and singing; at times, as in the highly carnivalesque *Doctor Sax,* orality and anality are implicitly linked. Genitality enters his work through (among other things) frequent references to the promiscuous sexual relations that were a hectic part of his life as a young adult; there is also a good deal of childhood sexuality in *Doctor Sax,* which has early experiences with masturbation and homosexuality among its many concerns. Still, its oral and anal interests are even stronger. The grotesque (and often media-inspired) characterizations in this novel include the title character, based partly on Fields and partly on "The Shadow" of radio and magazine fame, prized by Kerouac for his orally extravagant "Mwee hee hee ha ha" laugh; the baneful Wizard Faustus, a "Master of Earthly Evil" with a "moveable jaw-bird beak" and front teeth that are "missing" on page 50 but in need of cleaning by the Wizard's own "sensual tongue" on page 51; and Count Condu, who is a vampire and therefore belongs to the most orally insatiable (and insatiably oral) category of horror-movie monsters. Food also plays a strong part in the book, as does the color brown, which takes on a complex role associated with excrement, with the transformation of decayed matter into new organic life, and ultimately (as critic Gerald Nicosia points out) with what Samuel Taylor Coleridge calls "Life-in-Death."[21]

This trajectory begins to gather momentum in an early passage where the narrator, young Jackie Duluoz, remembers what he calls his Great Bathrobe Vision, which came to him while

> sitting in my mother's arms in a brown aura of gloom sent up by her bathrobe—it has cords hanging, like the cords in movies, bellrope for Catherine Empress, but brown, hanging around the bathrobe belt—the bathrobe of the family, I saw it for 15 or 20 years—that people were sick in . . . the brown of the color of life, the color of the brain, the gray brown brain, and the first color I noticed after the rainy grays of my first views of the world in the spectrum from the crib so dumb. . . . I am the pudding, winter is the gray mist. A shudder of joy ran through me—when I read of Proust's teacup—all those saucers in a crumb—all of History by thumb—all of a city in a tasty crumb—I got all my boyhood in vanilla winter waves around the kitchen stove. It's exactly like cold milk on hot bread pudding, the meeting of hot and cold is a hollow hole between memories of childhood.[22]

Here mother and child form an interconnected union of contradictions and complements (old-young, female-male, outside-inside, etc.) that is not closed and completed but intertwines within itself as well as interconnecting with the world of things, of people, of movies. Its associations in the protagonist's mind with early-childhood brownness—of life-organicism, brains-thought, food-nourishment—anticipate later immersions in the brownnesses of death, decay, and rebirth, linked with objects and places as diverse as a "swimbeach . . . where regularly you saw lumps of human shit floating," the "gloomy special brown Technicolor interior of my house," a "muddy brown pool . . . joyous to the test of squatting kids . . . as dewy and mornlike as brown mud water can get,—with its reflected brown taffy clouds," and a dangerously swelling river with "brown foam fury waters . . . thundering in midstream in one lump bump like the back of a carnival Caterpillar pitching green muslin-hunks and people screaming inside. . . ."[23] A high point comes when Doctor Sax counsels Jackie not to fear dying because "all and every moment is yearning to stay grown to you even as the pee-rade passes it—you'll take up your place in the hierarchal racks of vegetabalized [*sic*] heaven with a garland of carrots in your hair . . . in your death you'll know the *death* part of your life. And re-gain all that green, and browns."[24]

Oblivion and fecundity mingle with carnivalesque flamboyance in such passages. Kerouac's investment in the physical often serves a symbolic function, but it always maintains an emphatically concrete quality rooted in his own sense of bodily reality. He shares with Bakhtin a hearty respect for the lower body, and a conviction that—as Bakhtin puts it, paraphrasing Rabelais's priestess of the Holy Bottle—the "riches hidden in this underground . . . are superior to all that is in heaven, on the surface of the earth, or in the seas and rivers. True wealth and abundance are not on the highest or medium level [of the metaphorical body] but only in the lower stratum,"[25] whence the head of intellect is at its farthest remove, and excretion and copulation reign supreme.

Food, Photos, Fog

Kerouac's affinity with the dialogically grotesque, carnivalistic, and material erupts more robustly still in *Visions of Cody,* again narrated by Duluoz, now old enough to be called Jack rather than Jackie but as direct a Kerouac surrogate as ever.[26] The tone is established early in the novel with a boldly cinematic description (mimicking a lengthy tracking shot) of Hector's Cafeteria in New York, featuring an astonishing cascade of food-related imagery from "great rows of diced mint jellos in glasses . . . cherry jellos topp'd with whipcream . . . vast baked apples . . . grapes, pale green and brown . . . enormously dark chocolate cake (gleaming scatological brown) . . . lady fingers sticking up" to "white bottles of rich mad milk . . . the bread bun mountain . . . coffee counter, the urns, the cream jet, the steam . . . pink lovely looking lox . . . egg salads big enough for a giant," not to mention "deepdish strudel, of time and the river" and "that shining glazed sweet counter—showering like heaven—an all-out promise of joy in the great city of kicks."[27] This description strongly evokes the carnival tradition of feasts, banquets, and cornucopia, here found in the commodified form given to it by modern consumer society. Ginsberg calls the passage a "Homeric Hymn,"[28] and Weinreich traces the progression of its symbolic imagery from evocations of Edenic nature and paradise to suggestions of humanity's fall, indications of collapse and death, and finally a renewed aspiration toward paradise. A thoroughgoing ambivalence reigns as the passage oscillates between expansion and limitation,[29] all focalized through "[p]oor Cody, in front of this in his scuffled-up beat Denver shoes, his literary 'imitation' suit he had wanted to wear to be acceptable in New York cafeterias which he thought would be brown and plain like Denver cafeterias, with ordinary food. . . ."[30]

This section is a heroic but hardly unique portion of a novel wherein even passing references may find biology, mythology, scatology, and theology jangling against one another—as when Duluoz riffs out an acknowledgement that "all my life I've dreamed on breasts (and of course thighs, but now we're talking of breasts, hold your Venus, we're talking about Mars, and your water, we're talking about milk)—the dirty magazines of boyhood become the religious publications of manhood. . . ." The reference here is to a photograph described as "a pix of Ruth Maytime (the famous Hollywood actress)," with which Jack Duluoz becomes infatuated precisely because it is a simulacrum and therefore a suitable site for the projection of fantasies and lusts generated by his own corporeality. "I can hardly think or control myself—I even know this [gazing at the photo] is infinitely more delicious than touching Ruth's breast itself (though I'd do anything for the chance)," he declares. Later he adds that the photo's lack of color further enhances its sexual "reality" since he "was brought up in the balconies of B-movie theaters."[31]

The filmic allusions in such passages as this and the Great Bathrobe Vision of *Doctor Sax*—with its evocation of Marlene Dietrich in Josef von Sternberg's great movie *The Scarlet Empress* (1934), conjured up by the sash of a mother's cloak—are deliberate and revealing, pointing to movies as an ideal (and idealized) site for grotesque-body imagery. This idealization of movies reflects Kerouac's commitment to the conversion of thought (i.e., writerly imagination) into the physicality of prose modeled less upon traditional literary conceits than upon musical, painterly, and cinematic precedents.

The bodily image in cinema has rich potential for grotesquerie, since it lacks such real-world properties as solidity, three-dimensionality, and perceptibility by the "non-distance" senses of touch, taste, and smell. Kerouac recognizes this with particular acuteness in *Visions of Cody* when he describes the spectacle of Joan Crawford performing an on-location movie scene (which he inadvertently ran across in San Francisco one evening) and spins from it the simulacrum-upon-simulacrum of his "Joan Rawshanks in the Fog" improvisation, another key component of the *Visions of Cody* tapestry. Here he blows manic riffs that echo and parody cinematic procedure, as when he describes

> the great silence of the great moment of Hollywood, the actual TAKE (how many producers got high on Take do you think?) just as in a bullfight, when the moment comes for the matador to stick his sword into the bull and kill it . . . the actual moment, the central kill, the riddled middle idea, the thing, the Take, the actual juice suction of the camera catching a vastly planned action, the moment when we all know that the camera is germinating, a thing is being born whether we planned it right or not; there were three takes of every area of the action; Joan rushing up the drive, then Joan fiddling with her keys at the door, and later a third take that I never got to see, three shots of each, each shot carefully forewarned; and the exact actual moment of the Take is when silence falls over just like a bullfight.[32]

It is fascinating to observe Kerouac's wry reportage of the meticulous preplanning required for each take—exactly the sort of preplanning that he refused for his own work, including this novel. Meanwhile, his descriptions of Crawford-Rawshanks oscillate between the personally particular and the socially general, as when he feels

> a twinge of sorriness for Joan, either because all this time she'd been suffering real horrors nevertheless as movie queen that I had no idea about, or, in the general materialism of Hollywood she is being maltreated as a star "on the way out"; which she certainly is not at this moment (probably is), though of course all the teenage girls were quick to say, in loud voices for everyone to hear, that her makeup was very heavy, she'd practically have to stagger under it, and leaving it up to us to determine how saggy and baggy her face; well, naturally, I didn't expect Joan Crawfish in the fog to be anything but Joan Crawfish in the fog. . . .[33]

Nor does he overlook the speech mannerisms of director and star. The former jabbers about "what I've been trying to explain to Schultz for ten minutes, the meaneander there when you come in at the end byazacking along the trull, I told him and he won't listen, we called Red, it's absolutely—got the rest straight though?" Rawshanks replies, "Yes and tell Rogeroo to make room for me at the other end; o those horrible bores in there." And all this is accompanied by Kerouac's own sound track, magisterially evoked in prose, "as a buoy in the bay goes b-o, as a buoy in the bag goes b-o, bab-o, as a buoy in the bag goes bab-o. . . ."[34]

The grotesque, uproarious artificiality that characterizes Hollywood's relationship with its workers, its audience, its sociocultural context, and its ambivalent chroniclers has rarely been more crisply conjured than in this lengthy arabesque on a movie star who is

> actually in the fog, but as we can see with our own everyday eyes in the fog all lit by kleig lights, and in a furcoat story now, and not really frightened or anything but the central horror we all feel for her when she turns her grimace of horror on the crowd preparatory to running up the ramp, we've seen that face, ugh, she turns it away herself and rushes on with the scene, for a moment we've all had a pang of disgust, the director however seems pleased; he sucks on his red lollipop.[35]

Fortunately, outside this mist-enshrouded set there is a real America that refuses to be forgotten, and in the end Kerouac knows it will prevail. "At dawn," he tells us, "when Joan Rawshanks sees the first hints of great light over Oakland, and there swoops the bird of the desert, the fog will be gone."[36]

The Baroque Period of the Three Stooges

> But the latest and perhaps really, next to Mexico and the jazz tea high . . . best, vision, also on high, but under

> entirely different circumstances, was the vision I had of Cody as he showed me one drowsy afternoon . . . what and how the Three Stooges are like when they go staggering and knocking each other down the street, Moe, Curly (who's actually the bald domed one, big husky) and meaningless goof (though somewhat mysterious as though he was a saint in disguise, a masquerading superduper witch doctor with good intentions actually)—can't think of his name; Cody knows his name, the bushy feathery haired one.
>
> —Kerouac, *Visions of Cody*

Perhaps the most explosive combination of cinematic and grotesque-body aesthetics in all of Kerouac's work is the same novel's masterful aria on the Three Stooges, whose surreal antics become all the more phantasmic when—in a clever extension of the appearance-reality ambivalence found in the passage on the Ruth Maytime photo—he considers the comedy trio not as illusory shadows on a screen but as corporeal beings in the realm of the actual.

"Supposing the Three Stooges were real?" he asks with disarming directness. Then he envisions them springing to life at Cody's side, and almost instantly his prose takes on the crude, exhilarating physicality of their crude, exhilarating identities:

> Moe the leader, mopish, mowbry, mope-mouthed, mealy, mad, hanking, making the others quake; whacking Curly on the iron pate, backhanding Larry (who wonders); picking up a sledgehammer, honk, and ramming it down nozzle first on the flatpan of Curly's skull, boing, and all big dumb convict Curly does is muckle and yukkle and squeal, pressing his lips, shaking his old butt like jelly, knotting his Jell-o fists, eyeing Moe, who looks back and at him with that lowered and surly "Well what are you gonna do about it?" under thunderstorm eyebrows like the eyebrows of Beethoven, completely ironbound in his surls, Larry in his angelic or rather he really looks like he conned the other two to let him join the group, so they

> had to pay him all these years a regular share of the salary to them who work so hard with the props. . . .[37]

As in the Three Stooges' own work—and work by some other film artists, such as the surrealist Luis Buñuel and the body-intensive Jerry Lewis—outrageous escalation is one of Kerouac's basic strategies here: "it gets worse and worse, it started on an innocent thumbing, which led to backhand, then the pastries, then the nose yanks, blap, bloop, going, going, gong. . . ." The setting also undergoes expressive changes, from "the street right there in front of the Station" to "a sticky dream set in syrup universe" and then "an underground hell of their own invention." Yet the reality of these Stooges is insisted upon: "like Cody and me [they] were going to work, only they forget about that, and tragically mistaken and interallied, begin pasting and cuffing each other at the employment office desk as clerks stare; supposing in real gray day and not the gray day of movies and all those afternoons we spent looking at them . . . you saw them coming down Seventh Street looking for jobs—as ushers, insurance salesmen. . . ." And finally, looking at the notion of Stooge-Reality from yet another perspective, Kerouac acknowledges them as performers but takes *this* actuality as an ironic counterpoint to their on-screen personas:

> they are photographed in Hollywood by serious crews . . . until . . . they've been at it for so many years in a thousand climactic efforts superclimbing and worked out every refinement of bopping one another so much that now, in the end, if it isn't already over, in the baroque period of the Three Stooges they are finally bopping mechanically and sometimes so hard it's impossible to bear (wince), but by now they've learned not only how to master the style of the blows but the symbol and acceptance of them also, as though inured in their souls and of course long ago in their bodies, to buffetings and crashings in the rixy gloom of Thirties movies and B short subjects . . . the Stooges don't feel the blows any more, Moe is iron, Curly's dead,

> Larry's gone, off the rocker, beyond the hell and gone, (so ably hidden by his uncombable mop, in which, as G. J. used to say, he hid a Derringer pistol), so there they are, bonk, boing. . . .[38]

From these spectacles of Stoogeish grotesquerie, Cody derives a deep and comforting insight, realizing that "all the goofs he felt in him were justified in the outside world and he had nothing to reproach himself for, bonk, boing, crash, skittely boom, pow, slam, bang, boom, wham, blam, crack, frap, kerplunk, clatter, clap, blap, fap, slapmap, splat, crunch, crowsh, bong, splat, splat, *BONG!*" Cody's consolation is not a result of mere amusement at the Stooges' antics, or of mere diversion from the cares and conflicts that torment him. It derives rather from the Stooges' embodiment and exemplification—for Cody and for Kerouac himself—of two of the most potent transcendental possibilities to be found in Kerouac's universe. One is the ability of art to summon and sustain the most profound passions with which the human spirit is capable of communing; the Stooges do not simply caper and cavort, but in the untrammeled madness of their improvisations they provide "scenes for wild vibrating hysterias as great as the hysterias of hipsters at Jazz at the Philharmonics."

The other is the ability of the (finite) human spirit to penetrate the realm of the (divine) transhuman spirit through the most appalling throes of materiality. "Larry, goofhaired, mopplelipped, lisped, muxed and completely flunk—trips over a pail of whitewash and falls face first on a seven-inch nail that remains imbedded in his eyebone," Duluoz reports with matter-of-fact respect for this extreme instance of earthly suffering, endured by the very Stooge whose name he had forgotten a short time earlier. And then, astonishingly, he continues:

> the eyebone's connected to the shadowbone, shadowbone's connected to the luck bone, luck bone's connected to the, foul bone, foul bone's connected to the, high bone, high bone's connected to the, air bone, air bone's con-

> nected to the, sky bone, sky bone's connected to the, angel bone, angel bone's connected to the, God bone, *God bone's connected to the bone bone. . . .*[39]

As wildly carnivalesque figures whose relationship to "real" character types is tenuous at best and whose "real" existence for Kerouac transpired wholly on movie screens—he saw Joan Crawford behind the scenes but never this crazy trio—the Three Stooges are perfect grotesqueries, capable of executing any irrationality, surviving any torment, sustaining any transfiguration that may come their way. Kerouac's trajectory for Larry's ultimate adventure begins with a Rabelaisian linkage of incongruities—eye to bone, bone to shadow—and then proceeds to an inversion of the conventionally proper (foul connects to high) and a transcendence of the materially possible (bone connects to God). Most audacious in this itemization of Larry's spiritual anatomy is its circularity, foreshadowing the cyclical configuration of Kerouac's novelistic oeuvre as it culminates its own escalating ethereality (air-to-sky-to-angel-to-God) with a return to earthly, obdurate bone. This return is doubly affirmed *(bone bone)* in its ineluctable corporeality, yet wholly transformed by its contextualization in a catalogue of sublimely grotesque body parts.

Bardo Follies

> There where it smells of shit
> it smells of being.
>
> —Antonin Artaud, *To Have Done with the Judgment of God*

> . . . if the . . . deceased is not properly prepared, and who is?, to meet the conditions of that bloody bloodless Bardo Plane, the Astral Realm to which his own subconscious will attune him, that particular portion of Purgatory region where until next incarnation, if earthbound, as is usually the unhappy case, he'll emotionally burn away the drearer dross, or if high bound . . . reap the dearer dreams of his Divine desires. . . .
>
> —Neal Cassady, 1959 letter

Observing that the sound of one's own voice is heard largely through bone conduction, media theorist Douglas Kahn notes that the phonographically reproduced voice "returns to its parent through air conduction, that is, without the bones. The phonographed selfsame voice is deboned." Kahn concludes that such deboning constitutes "a machine-critique of Western metaphysics" since it "uproots an experiential centerpiece for sustaining notions of the presence of the voice—hearing oneself speak—and moves the selfsame voice from its sacrosanct location into the contaminating realms of writing, society, and afterlife."[40]

This point about phonography cannot be transferred directly to discourse about cinema, because visual reflections (in mirrors, etc.) have always been comparatively accessible and familiar (sonic echoes are a weak sensory competitor for them) and because the anatomical apparatus for vision is configured quite differently from that employed in hearing.[41] It remains true, however, that Kerouac's unremitting fascination with *precisely* the realms of writing, society, and afterlife led him to divine—on the "real" movie screens of B-movie theaters and the phantasmic "movie screens" of his own propulsively visual imagination—a sublimated Stooge whose haplessly punctured eyebone opens on a vision that simultaneously accepts and transcends the human condition in all its ambiguous *écriture,* carnivalistic sociality, and yearning for redemption in a beyond at which even the inspired irrationality of a Stooge and Kerouac combined can only dimly hint.

Points of intersection among hysteria, corporeality, and phonography are familiar terrain for Antonin Artaud, who was famously prone to glossolalia, a nonreferential speech form—often associated with the mentally ill, the spiritually possessed, and the very young—that transforms language into a string of impenetrable signifiers, repudiating all meaning and valorizing the unadulterated voice. A notable instance is found at the beginning of his great 1947 radio play, *To Have Done with the Judgment of God:*

kré Everything **puc te**
kré must be arranged **puk te**
pek to a hair **li le**
kré in a fulminating **pek ti le**
e order. **kruk**
pte[42]

Kerouac was also fascinated with vocal sound (and its graphological transcription) as a material substance stripped of conventional signification. Excellent examples appear at the end of his novel *Big Sur* in the appended poem "Sea," which takes its inspiration from noises of the ocean, as in this excerpt.

Clock——Clack——Milk——
Mai! mai! mai! ma!
says the wind blowing sand——
Pluto eats the sea——
Ami go———da——che pop
Go——Come——Cark——
Care——Kee ter da vo
Kataketa pow! Kek kek kek!
Kwakiutl! Kik!
Some of theserather taratasters
trapped hyra tchere thaped
the anadondak ram ma lat
round by Krul to Pat the lat
rat the anaakakalked
romon t o t t e k
Kara VOOOM
frup——[43]

Like these syllables, the catalogues of onomatopoetic Stooge-abuse in *Visions of Cody* have the musicated ring of Artaud's raving glossolalia.[44] Kerouac's evocation of Larry's dematerialized-rematerialized bones also carries the reader into an Artaudian domain, recalling the French writer's ruminations on the convulsively reconfigured body, as in this crucial passage from *To Have Done with the Judgment of God:*

> In order to exist you need only let yourself go until you
> are,
> but in order to live
> you must be somebody,
> in order to be somebody,
> you must have a bone,
> not be afraid of showing the bone,
> and of losing the meat on the way.[45]

The nonplace that Artaud mentally inhabited in his later mad years appeared to him as the realm of Bardo, a liminal territory identified by ancient Tibetan theology as the home of the soul during the forty-nine days between bodily death and rebirth. Artaud describes Bardo in *Artaud le Mômo* as "the pang of death into which the self falls with a splash."[46] For his electroshocked psyche, this territory represents a natural destination for the "body without organs" that he prescribes as a corrective for humanity's ills in the valedictory portion of *To Have Done with the Judgment of God:*

> Man is sick because he is badly constructed.
> We must decide to strip him in order to scratch
> out this animalcule which makes him itch to death,
>
> god,
> and with god
> his organs.
>
> For tie me down if you want to,
> but there is nothing more useless than an organ.
>
> When you have given him a body without organs,
> then you will have delivered him from all his
> automatisms
> and restored him to his true liberty.

> Then you will teach him again to dance inside out
> as in the delirium of our accordion dance halls
> and that inside out will be his true side out.[47]

Artaud associated this deconstructed *corps à l'envers* with the invisible spaces of the radiophonic airwaves.[48] Yet the paramorphic freedom and grandiose grotesquerie of the body without organs might also be situated in the hyperrealist realm of cinematic simulacra. In cinema, the skeptical Artaud found only a limited "poetry of contingency, the poetry of what might be."[49] Still, he experimented with film during his artistic career, and he perceived its capacity for deorganicizing the stuff of life:

> Cinema exalts matter and reveals it to us in its profound spirituality, in its relations with the spirit from which it has emerged. Images are born, are derived from one another purely as images, impose an objective synthesis more penetrating than any abstraction, create worlds which ask nothing of anyone or anything. But out of this pure play of appearances, out of this so to speak transubstantiation of elements is born an inorganic language that moves the mind by osmosis and without any kind of transposition in words. And because it works with matter itself, cinema creates situations that arise from the mere collision of objects, forms, repulsions, attractions. It does not detach itself from life but rediscovers the original order of things. . . . A cinema which is studded with dreams, and which gives you the physical sensation of pure life, finds its triumph in the most excessive form of humor. A certain excitement of objects, forms, and expressions can only be translated into the convulsions and surprises of a reality that seems to destroy itself with an irony in which you can hear a scream from the extremities of the mind.[50]

Despite his conclusion that "cinema remains a fragmentary and . . . stratified and frozen . . . conquest of reality,"[51] and despite his eventual abandonment of even radio as an expressive medium,[52] Artaud appears to have suspected that from the radiating surfaces of film might conceivably spring the supremely superficial body of which he dreamed—in the formulation of audiophonist Gregory Whitehead, a body "rolling on some stunning ground" (like Captain Ahab, whose "whole beaten brain seems as beheaded") and quoting *Artaud le Mômo*'s late chant:

> The
> world,
> but it's no longer me.
> And what do you care,
> says Bardo,
>   it's me.[53]

The existential limbo between me and not-me, and the performative limbo between not-me and not-not-me,[54] are territories of liminality that the Beat writers found haunted with dark beauties and daunting possibilities. Gilles Deleuze and Félix Guattari recognize this when they list Kerouac and Ginsberg among Anglo-American authors who "know how to leave, to scramble the codes, to cause flows to circulate, to traverse the desert of the body without organs" yet simultaneously "never cease failing" to complete a transgressive project dogged by the demons of its age. "Never has delirium oscillated more between its two poles," the philosophers conclude, lamenting the closures of "neurotic impasse . . . exotic territorialities . . . or worse still, an old fascist dream."[55]

Kerouac's longing for order, tenderness, and piety bears out his centrality to an American literature whose destiny is, Deleuze and Guattari suggest, "crossing limits and frontiers, causing deterritorialized flows of desire to circulate, but also always making these flows transport fascisizing, moralizing, Puritan, and familialist territorialities."[56] To acknowledge Kerouac's turbulent "oscillations of the unconscious," however, is not to slight the ecstatic revolutionism that erupted from the best, most paradoxical intuitions of his Bardo-bound spirit.

Artaud reached that sublimely metaphysicized realm before him, and—grotesquely and incredibly—so did the Three Stooges, at least the way Kerouac tells it. Jackie Duluoz was perceptive when he called the Proustian meeting of hot and cold a hollow hole between memories of childhood; but it takes the older, wiser Jack Duluoz to decode those differentials of molecular motion into dialogic poles of existence and oblivion, potentiality and void, life in death and death in life; and to apprise cold-war America of the liberating news that History's carnivalesque contravisions may travel a nail-poked route to revelation through organless film-bodies like Larry the Stooge.

DESOLATION ANGELS: KEROUAC, BUDDHISM, AND FILM

Paradox, ambiguity, and irrationality were important to all the key figures of the Beat Generation group, including Jack Kerouac, who cultivated "first thought best thought" writing techniques meant to draw on deep and largely inaccessible levels of the subconscious mind. Related to this practice of "spontaneous bop prosody" were Kerouac's longtime involvements with two other areas of interest. One was Buddhism, which he discovered while prowling the Columbia University library during his student days.[1] The other was cinema, which attracted him both as a moviegoer and as an adventurous artist who wasn't above dreams of going to Hollywood and making great films while purging the place of its decadent commercialism.

Cinema makes only intermittent appearances in Kerouac's books, but on these occasions it serves as a polyvalent concept with a variety of descriptive, metaphoric, analogical, and practical uses. Passages in the 1965 novel *Desolation Angels* illustrate the usefulness of this concept for Kerouac, while demonstrating how his unorthodox writing methods generate modalities of consciousness and meaning with few parallels outside works by members of the Beat group.[2] The following analysis is not intended to posit firm connections or to multiply far-flung comparisons among diverse literary, cinematic, and religious notions; rather, it means to suggest in an allusive manner the sorts of heterogeneous interactions that took place within Kerouac's imagination as he wrestled with conundrums and ambivalences that preoccupied him both personally and professionally.

Impermanence

Desolation Angels is a peripatetic novel that follows Jack Duluoz, a Kerouac surrogate, through a long series of travels, encounters, and adventures. It begins with Duluoz seeking meditative bliss through a job as fire lookout on a Pacific Northwest mountaintop, where his initial romance with isolation turns into an overwhelming itchiness that speeds him back to the ordinary world. Subsequent journeys take him to a variety of places ranging from San Francisco and New York to Tangiers and London, and finally to New York, where he bids goodbye to the Beat life and settles into "peaceful sorrow at home" marked by a poignant blend of tranquility and disillusionment.

At one point in the novel's second part, subtitled "Desolation in the World," the word *movie* takes on three different meanings in three consecutive appearances within fewer than ten pages.

Passage A: In the first instance, the interwoven (non)entities of God and the universe are described as "just nothing but Infinity infinitely variously amusing itself with a movie, empty space and matter both, it doesnt limit itself to either one, infinitude wants all." This passage suggests that human experience and indeed all material existence ("the murder and the useless activity") are a spectacle endlessly constructed and consumed by the impersonal "maddening void which doesnt care what we do."

Passage B: In the second instance, which presents a substantial connotative shift, mountain-dwelling Duluoz gazes at a panorama so "ephemeral" and "evanescent" as to seem ineffable and fundamentally transvisual, charged with a "heartbreaking mystery" that makes him realize "it's a God-game (for me) and I see the movie of reality as a vanishment of sight in a pool of liquid understanding." Here existence is evoked in metacinematic terms, as a film that elides physical sight in favor of spiritual insight.

Passage C: In the third instance, a moment of crisis for Duluoz fixes a single obsessive idea—"I can't make it"—as "my only thought as I keep going, which thought is like phosphorescent negative red glow imprinting the film of my brain. . . ." Here the cinematic trope has an anatomical (brain-film) connection; yet it exceeds mere biological description, as pure ideation makes its "tracing" on what might be called the thought-sensitive emulsion of the protagonist's psyche.

The variations in tone, sense, and meaning from each of these cinema tropes to the others may be construed as radical polysemy or mere semiotic slippage on Kerouac's part, depending on one's view of him as a sophisticated pioneer of spontaneous stylistics or (in author Truman Capote's famous formulation) simply a prolific typist. A strong case can be made, however, that such deployments of cinema-related concepts are deliberate in their instability, since cinema is in Kerouac's view a paradoxically precise metaphor for a fundamentally imprecise phenomenon: the "impermanence" of the human condition that constitutes one of the Three Marks of Existence in the Buddhist belief system that played an important part in his intellectual and spiritual life. Beat poet Allen Ginsberg claims that Kerouac was not a dabbler or dilettante in Buddhist lore but became a "brilliant intuitive Buddhist scholar" with a "learned grasp" of Eastern thought.[3] Buddhism was also influential on a number of Western authors—including the Transcendentalist thinkers Ralph Waldo Emerson and Henry David Thoreau, and the historian Oswald Spengler[4]—who in turn influenced Kerouac and other Beat writers. So it is not surprising that Kerouac developed links between "book-movie" tropes, to borrow a term from his novel *Doctor Sax: Faust Part*

Three, and Buddhist concepts that were central to his thinking throughout a major portion of his career.[5]

Ginsberg credits Kerouac with a profound understanding of impermanence in the Buddhist sense, which Ginsberg defines as "the transitoriness of our condition; the fact that what we have here is like a dream, in the sense that it is real while it is here." That is to say, Kerouac had "the sense of the reality of existence and at the same time the unreality of existence," and therefore grasped what Buddhism calls the "co-immergent wisdom" which holds that "this universe is real, and at the same time unreal . . . form and emptiness are identical." This is related to another Buddhist concept, found within the set of axioms known as the Four Noble Truths: that since our existence is best seen (in Eastern terms) as an open space teeming with possibilities rather than (in Western terms) as a domain of imprisoning darkness, "it is possible to appreciate the aesthetic play of forms in emptiness, and to exist in this place like majestic kings of our own consciousness," in Ginsberg's words. Rejecting the existentialist notion of the void as a "claustrophobic bummer," Kerouac embraced instead the Zen notion of the void as "'open space' or 'accommodating space.'"[6] Armed with this peace-producing *sunyata,* or "wisdom of emptiness,"[7] he developed a tendency to celebrate multiple forms of vastness and spaciousness, and nurtured a "panoramic" sensibility in which Ginsberg finds cinematic properties. Manifestations of this sensibility include the end of Kerouac's first novel, *The Town and the City* (1950), with its vision of a football field and a setting sun, and his numerous descriptions of a figure in a public space "with the camera receding as it does at the end of the movie *Les Enfants du Paradise* [1945] when the camera recedes above the buildings, above the Ferris wheel, until we see the vast crowd receding in a much vaster space."[8]

Equally related to Buddhist thinking is Kerouac's fascination with spontaneity in art, music, and literature. "If you are now desirous of more perfectly understanding Supreme Enlightenment," he quotes from the *Surangama Sutra* in a late essay, "you must learn to answer spontaneously and with no recourse to discriminate thinking." He adds that "spontaneous, or ad lib, artistic writing imitates as best it can the flow of the mind as it moves in its space-time continuum. . . . To break through the barrier of language with WORDS, you have to be in orbit around your mind. . . ."[9] The latter phrase vividly suggests the ideal of standing at a distance from the self (and repudiating the self as a unitary being) that is so important to Beat creativity.

Interfusion

Kerouac appears to have regarded the stream of images in cinema as a dematerialized and hence ungraspable phenomenon that constitutes a natural analogue for three other phenomena in which he was deeply interested: the flow of human mental processes, the flow of spontaneous prose that captures and represents those processes, and the flow of change and "becoming" that Buddhism postulates as the processual foundation of the material universe. The last-mentioned concept is related to the Sanskrit term *samsara,* which signifies the "world of becoming" in Buddhist thought—that is, the entire physical and mental universe, all of which is governed by eternal laws of cause and effect. Since the universe is an eternally dynamic matrix of interdependent forces, it is characterized by *anicca* or impermanence, whereby everything from physical objects to human thoughts and feelings is temporary, destined to be replaced by something new that it helped to create.[10] The quest for quiescence or immovability is carried out in Buddhism by an attempt to fuse "consciousness of change and impermanence . . . with an unconscious consciousness of eternity, unchangeability or timelessness," as Buddhist scholar Daisetz Teitaro Suzuki puts it. Buddhist terminology equates this complementary "interfusion of consciousness and unconsciousness" with interfusion of "the Many and the One . . . Form and Emptiness . . . Distinction (or Discrimination) and Non-Distinction (or Non-Discrimination)," and it is this fusion of seeming opposites that may be designated the "philosophy" of Buddhism in the Zen form that influenced Kerouac and like-minded Beats.[11]

Kerouac's association of Buddhist concepts with cinematic analogues and metaphors proves to be a productive synthesis. Dynamism and flux are primary characteristics of film expression, and Buddhism holds the same qualities to be inherent in all experience and existence. The clearest manifestation of cinematic dynamism is montage, the arrangement of signifiers into differential relationships along a syntagmatic axis. Here is an echo of what Buddhism calls "impermanence," in that no single shot of a film (at least within the "classical" film style and its most common variants) may accrete a disproportionate duration of its own but must give way to the images that succeed it within the spatial limitations of the screen and the temporal limitations of the film's overall length. Furthermore, every shot carries within itself a "potential montage," to use philosopher Gilles Deleuze's formulation, and every "movement-image" is actually a "matrix or cell of time," since change is a function of "the objects between which movement is established." Hence, time in classical cinema depends on movement via montage.[12] The medium for such change is the spectator's perception, since the differential object relationships that are interwoven so completely with cinematic time have no meaning *as* relationships except as they are comprehended by the viewer in the act of watching the film. Indeed, the fact of continual image succession means that no film has more than a part-object existence at any given moment except in the mind of the spectator who consumes each image, retains its meanings in memory, and assembles those meanings into a more or less coherent whole.[13] Here is another link with the Buddhist thought that influenced Kerouac, since the idea of diversified image matrices converging within the spectator's mind to form a new order of meaning recalls the Buddhist doctrine that the search for understanding requires the individual to maintain a hold on different and often conflicting modalities of existence.

Dreams

Kerouac's association of cinema with the Buddhist concept of interfusion may be attributed, then, to his interest in sustaining disparate modes of thought and meaning within his own mental life, and to the congruence he detected between specific properties of film and sweeping properties of existence itself as construed by Buddhist thought.[14] While it is impossible to recoup Kerouac's thought processes beyond the tracings they have left within his highly intuitive prose, these tracings suggest connections that might have played a part (however subconscious and subliminal) in the poetics of *Desolation Angels.*

The states of *multiplicity* (the vast) and *singularity* (the immediate) within the cosmos (related to the God-game and reality-movie references in passage B above) are echoed in cinema by the *diversity of images* within a classical film and the *unity of impression* that such a film attempts to convey within the spectator's consciousness. The states of *form* (the perceptible) and *emptiness* (the void) within the universe (related to the tension between Infinity and movie in passage A) are echoed by the *light-figures of filmic spectacle* and the *instants of darkness* that separate their fleeting appearances upon the underlying blankness of the screen, which is a site for what Ginsberg calls "the aesthetic play of forms in emptiness," themselves as illusory as they are ephemeral. The states of *reality* and *unreality* (related to the pairing of brain and ideation in passage C) are echoed by (on one hand) the efforts of conventional cinema to *represent, signify, or fix the realm of material existence* and (on the other) the qualities of *transience, intangibility, and conditionality* that persist in cinematic experience. These leaps of Kerouacian association may be summarized as follows:

Buddhist thought	**Cinematic discourse**
—multiplicity (the vast)	—diversity of images
—singularity (the immediate)	—unity of impression
—form (the perceptible)	—figuration (film frames)
—emptiness (the void)	—darkness (between frames)

—reality	—depiction of material existence
—unreality	—intangibility, contingency

Kerouac associated cinema not only with Buddhist insights but also with the state of dreaming, in which he found another fertile source of inspiration. "When I woke up from my sleep I just lay there looking at the pictures that were fading slowly like a movie fadeout into the recesses of my subconscious mind," he writes in the preface to his *Book of Dreams,* adding later that "the subconscious mind (the *manas* working thru from the *alaya-vijnana*) does not make any mental discriminations of good or bad, thisa or thata. . . ."[15] Cinema's oscillation between reality (which it claims to represent, either naturalistically or expressionistically) and unreality (which it can never escape, given the evanescence of its signifiers and the temporality of its structures) is related to the specifically dreamlike characteristics that have often been noted in accounts of film spectatorship.[16] It is a truism that dream states reduce distinctions between actuality and fantasy; to cite observations by Jacques Derrida, in dreams "the *totality* of sensory images is illusory," and the dreaming subject "is farther from true perception than the madman" since in sleep "the *absolute totality* of ideas of sensory origin becomes suspect" and is stripped of "objective value."[17] Given the compatibility among *(a)* the evanescence of cinematic representation, *(b)* the totalizing subjectivity of the dream state, and *(c)* the Buddhist concept of *sunyata* as an accommodating void that subsumes the real and unreal alike, one can imagine the appeal of cinema-derived figuration for an author struggling to conceive the cosmos, his tumultuous visions of it, and his suffering life within it as a synesthetic whole at once ephemeral and immanent. Language evocative of cinema must have seemed a natural choice for Kerouac in his radical attempts to capture the dreamlike, *sunyata*-infused ambiguity of his perceptions vis-à-vis illusion and actuality.

Pointing to the deliberate ambiguity that suffuses much of Kerouac's work, critic Regina Weinreich observes that he has a way of generalizing from the particular as if he were bringing his subject into focus through a camera lens. With reference to the (highly cinematic) statement in Kerouac's immensely complex novel *Visions of Cody* that at one point the "prime focal goal" of the novel's eponymous hero was "nothing less and nothing more than the redbrick wall behind the red neons," she notes that as "neon images give way to the solid structures of walls behind them . . . this lighting reveals a point of consciousness that is larger than the hero or any point in his universe," encapsulating tensions between appearance-reality and permanence-impermanence that underlie a large variety of oppositions in Kerouac's language and narrative constructions.[18]

What must be added to Weinreich's analysis is the fact that Kerouac's earnest Buddhism would not ultimately accept these oppositions *as* oppositions but would strive to realize their subsumption by the emptiness of *sunyata* and the fundamental insight that "form is emptiness, form is no different from emptiness, emptiness no different from form, form is the emptiness, emptiness is the form. Sensation, recognition, conceptualization, consciousness are also like this," to quote the *Prajnaparamita,* a work of great importance to the core Beat figures.[19] Even as he uses literature as a tool for exploring the exquisitely ambivalent realms of life and dream, Kerouac learns that art is not a pathway to privileged awareness but merely, in the words of biographer Gerald Nicosia, "another mirror of a reality inseparable from dream. . . . The only thing we know about these visions of life is that they end, that the void engulfs them. . . ."[20] Or, as Kerouac writes in his epic poem *Mexico City Blues,*

> Only awake to universal mind,
> accept everything,
> see everything,
> it is empty,
> Accept as thus—the Truth.[21]

REVISION, PREVISION, AND THE AURA OF IMPROVISATORY ART

In a 1958 essay about Jack Kerouac, whose novel *On the Road* had played a major role in putting the Beat Generation on the map of both mainstream and countercultural America a year earlier, Beat fellow traveler John Clellon Holmes imagined his friend working at his typewriter, "staring into the blankness of the space in front of him, careful not to *will* anything, and simply recording the 'movie' unreeling in his mind. . . . Somehow an open circuit of feeling had been established between his awareness and its object of the moment, and the result was as startling as being trapped in another man's eyes."[1]

Holmes appears to give an accurate account of Kerouac's working method here. Convinced as early as 1948 that "spontaneous writing" was the key to honest and authentic literary creation, Kerouac had refined this technique in 1951 after listening to the fluid "lyric-alto" style of jazz saxophonist Lee Konitz, deciding "to write the way [Konitz] plays."[2] Eight years later, in 1959, he published one of several manifestos in which he elaborated on the importance of an improvisatory writing meant to capture "the unspeakable visions of the individual" in unadulterated form; appearing in his fragmentary list of thirty "essentials" are such phrases as, "Write what you want bottomless from bottom of the mind," and, "Composing wild, undisciplined, pure, coming in from under, crazier the better."[3]

Philosophically, the view taken by Holmes and Kerouac of what the latter called "spontaneous bop prosody" and "spontaneous trance composition" is rooted in a romanticist sensibility or, in Friedrich Nietzsche's terminology, a Dionysian one. The emphasis is on immediacy, individuality, unpredictability, and freedom from sociocultural norms imposed by the present or inherited from the past.

This sensibility has been shared by many artists and critics who promulgate notions of improvisation as an idealized route to the authentic expression of a unique soul, spirit, or inner self. The assumption that ideals of spontaneity and authenticity are achievable through improvisation may be explicit, as when cornetist Jimmy McPartland states that his apprenticeship with a Chicago jazz group trained him to "play the way you feel, yourself" and when he recalls that legendary musician Bix Beiderbecke could not play the same chorus more than once because, in Beiderbecke's words, "I don't feel the same way twice. . . . I don't know what's going to happen next."[4] Or the assumption may be implicit, as when a reference work on jazz states that improvised music "gives the player an opportunity for self-expression which is to a large degree absent when he reproduces composed or arranged works."[5] In its supposition that "self" expression is facilitated less effectively by *interpretation* than by *invention*, and that the latter is singularly linked to such properties as "spontaneity, surprise, experiment, and discovery,"[6] this assertion tacitly endorses the concept of improvisation as a privileged means of access to "immediate flash material from the mind," in the words of Beat poet Allen Ginsberg, who shared Kerouac's interests in this area.[7]

Alongside the idea that improvising taps directly into the mind as "one continuous, vivid flow of sense-data, associations, memories and meditations,"[8] however, is a qualified view of the process that recognizes its connection with planning, deliberation, preconceptualization, and other mental activities that are not wholly spontaneous, individualistic, or autotelic in the ways suggested by idealized discourses of extemporaneous invention. In defining improvisation, for example, the jazz reference work cited above acknowledges that in addition to "the immediate composition of an entire work by its performers," the practice may alternatively involve "the elaboration or other variation of an existing framework" or may follow a course "in between" these possibilities.[9] Semantically, the affirmation that improvisatory work can operate on each of these levels (i.e., immediate composition and reworking of an existing framework) simply follows the dictionary definition of "improvise" as meaning both "to invent, compose, or perform with little or no preparation" and "to make or provide from available materials."[10] It is notable, however, that artists and critics often place their emphasis on the term's first meaning rather than its second. Indeed, the second is often presented as if it were an occasionally relevant modification of the first, treated as a mere afterthought or addendum, or altogether ignored.

The effect of this discursive maneuver is to ratify the links among improvisation, individuality, and authenticity put forth by many Beat writers, bebop musicians, and like-minded artists. Yet a look at the actual methodologies of some paradigmatic practitioners in these fields suggests that spur-of-the-moment creation may not be nearly as divorced from preconceived ideas, prerehearsed techniques, and prearranged effects as its advocates frequently appear to believe. This finding raises important questions related to the ontological nature as well as the day-to-day practice of improvisatory art.

Improvisational Mystique

Why have artists and critics allowed—or caused—such a mystique to grow around spur-of-the-moment creativity as a pathway to aesthetic and psychological authenticity? While improvisation has played a significant role in artistic creation for centuries—it was a favorite practice during the classical period of European music, to cite one of many possible examples—an important reason for its high reputation in the modernist era may be twentieth-century uncertainties regarding the authenticity of artistic works and practices themselves. Walter Benjamin casts light on this possibility when he introduces the term *aura* to identify certain qualities of the traditional artwork: its position within an established lineage, its situatedness in a particular time and place, and the "unique phenomenon of a distance" that it presents to the beholder no matter how physically close it may be. While the auratic effect has a long and imposing history, Benjamin argues that contemporary mass audiences have desires conducive to different results—the wish to bring things "closer," not just "spatially" but also "humanly," and the wish to overcome "the uniqueness of every reality" by according weight and significance to reproductions that displace the originals from which they are made. By facilitating the "decay" of art's auratic quality, such desires reveal what Benjamin finds a regrettable popular belief in the "universal equality" of perceptible things. In contrast, the auratic work remains "essentially distant" and "unapproachable" in its "unique existence," even if there is a degree of "closeness which one may gain from its subject matter."[11]

To focus on jazz again, it is interesting to observe how closely its early days happen to coincide with the birth of the recording industry, clearly a major event (along with the emergence of cinema) in the development of the age of mechanical reproduction.[12] For the first time, recording technology brought jazz and other forms of music—not in amateur varieties but in prestigious, professionally honed presentations—into homes, workplaces, and commercial establishments, thus taking the music physically *closer* to its consumers while contradicting its *uniqueness* via the ready availability of copies that are (actually) identical to one another and (putatively) indistinguishable from the original performances that they reproduce. Embraced with alacrity by large segments of the expanding turn-of-the-century market for consumer goods, this development hardly encouraged ongoing respect for such auratic qualities as unapproachability or time-and-place specificity. Some observers, eventually including Frankfurt School philosophers like Benjamin, responded to the reproducibility trend with growing uneasiness about the course that it would take in the hands of the capitalistic power brokers who controlled it. But the popular imagination, won over by the unprecedented plenitude of readily available cultural products, remained largely untroubled by such thoughts.

It is likely that the growth of mechanically reproduced performances played a role in the tendency of pre–World War II jazz musicians to stray from the improvisatory roots of their art—exemplified by the polyphonic New Orleans or Dixieland style—and steer jazz toward Europeanized models that undergirded another huge sector ("serious" or "concert" music) of the recording industry. In the twenties, to be sure, recordings facilitated the rising popularity of solo jazz improvisation by allowing one-time-only flights of invention to be readily and inexpensively heard and revisited by listeners. But in the thirties and forties, recordings may have paradoxically fostered the critical and commercial dominance of "swing" or "big band" styles that relied on large-scale instrumentation (which proved no more unwieldy in recording studios than in the upscale, predominantly white nightclubs that were boosting the economic fortunes of jazz) and used "through-composed" arrangements that downplayed improvisation but enabled commercial interests to exploit popular numbers with newfound efficiency. While big-band arrangements almost always left room for improvised solos and "breaks" by individual performers, these were subordinated to the prearranged number as a whole, carefully "charted" and rehearsed in advance.[13] The prestige of improvisation did not regain its early ground until the years immediately after World War II, when the innovative bop school reasserted extemporaneous playing as an essential jazz ingredient. Phonograph records then rose in importance once again, given the renewed interest in preserving unrepeatable solos—not only in terms of pitch, rhythm, and tempo but also of such notation-resistant qualities as tone, dynamics, and "mood."

The question that now arises is why such a highly improvisational style as bebop should successfully emerge when it did. Historians have suggested many valid answers to this, from the arrival of a postwar "fresh start" mentality to changes in music education among both players and listeners. But one underrecognized factor may be a nagging uneasiness over music's loss of auratic dignity during half a century of mechanical reproduction. In contrast to the marks of auratic authenticity noted in Benjamin's account—specificity, uniqueness, unapproachability—recording technology offers *(a)* the ability to hear a recorded piece with no regard for the time or place of its original performance, *(b)* the proliferation of endless copies easily obtained, and *(c)* a sense of not only physical proximity to the work ("a breathtaking performance in your own home") but also aesthetic intimacy ("the most subtle nuances") and even a sort of artistic communion ("you hear the full intentions of the composer") with its creator.[14] Improvisation offers a field on which such displacements of auratic qualities might be recouped in at least three ways:

1. Elements of singularity and "specialness" may be lost in reproduction, but they maintain their viability in live performances of improvised music, which provide a spur-of-the-moment "nowness" that recordings must lack by definition. Only a fraction of such performances can ever be recorded, moreover, which gives even their mass-marketed reproductions a certain secondhand cachet.

2. Live performances of *through-composed* music offer more singularity and "nowness" than recordings of such music do, but they suffer alongside live performances of *improvised* music in these respects, since unlike improvisations they can be repeated

as often as desired in substantially the same form. Most listeners know this, and they also know that recorded improvisations retain a greater degree of specificity than recordings of through-composed pieces do, since the improvisation was captured during its sole moment of existence; even record listeners uninterested in the original time-and-place particularities of an improvisation may value the fact that it was a singular occurrence rather than a representative run-through of a precisely notated piece that can be played many times with little variation.

3. The ability to craft, manipulate, and "improve" a performance via recording-studio technology puts a premium on off-the-cuff spontaneity, which may be regarded as a mark of intellectual alertness and emotional "cool" as well as creative ability and musical skill. (The player who improvises before a live audience or insists on direct, unmodified recording of a one-time-only performance may therefore be seen as the diametrical opposite of such a musician as classical pianist Glenn Gould, who took a radical stance *for* cut-and-splice studio recording and *against* all forms of live performance.)

These three points illustrate the value of improvisation as a tool for restoring to jazz auratic qualities that are threatened by the prevalence of phonographic reproduction. Hence they suggest a significant reason why many musicians and listeners felt a need to reinvest improvised music with a prestige that had dwindled during the big-band era; this need in turn suggests why claims for allegedly inherent traits of improvisation—authenticity, spontaneity, individuality—are often exaggerated or misrepresented by its advocates.

Bebop

To make this assertion is not to deny in any way that improvisation is a longstanding and productive form of creativity in jazz; it is only to note how apprehensions over authenticity, spontaneity, and individuality in music have encouraged the *discursive* maneuver of emphasizing certain idealized virtues of improvisation even as improvisatory *practice* draws on techniques of preparation and preconceptualization that were developed before such apprehensions ever had reason to take root.

Bebop is among the most fertile breeding grounds of improvisation, as commentary by insiders and outsiders alike has consistently stressed. Yet it is equally clear that bebop partakes of the secondary definition ("elaboration or other variation of an existing framework") as well as the primary definition ("immediate composition of an entire work by its performers") cited above. At issue here is the nearly ubiquitous bebop technique of using a familiar harmonic framework—often borrowed from a frequently performed "standard" or a current hit song—as a framing or orienting device for unfamiliar melodic and rhythmic inventions that are overlaid upon it.[15] The prominence of this method in bebop stems from the need for an organizing principle that *(a)* provides the musicians with a frame of reference that allows their improvisations to remain collectively as well as individually coherent no matter how adventurous or far-reaching they might become, and *(b)* anchors the listeners in intelligible aesthetic territory that helps them maintain their musical bearings and gives them the pleasure of a known commodity even if the improvisatory explorations head in difficult or bewildering directions. These needs explain the preference of many bop players for preselected chord progressions that are not just readily comprehensible but in many cases instantly recognizable to all involved.[16] In addition to these harmonic considerations, well-known melodies also contribute to bebop performances—played more or less straightforwardly during the first (thematic statement) and last (recapitulation) segments of a piece, and quoted (often humorously or sardonically) in the course of otherwise wide-ranging improvisations.

The expropriation of preexisting pop-culture elements is not bebop improvisation's only involvement with the elaboration of available materials as opposed to purely extemporaneous invention. Noting that the proliferation of freewheeling "jam sessions" allowed bop players "a forum in which to practice improvisation," cultural historian Daniel Belgrad points out that "practicing" and "improvising" need not be contradictory terms, since the latter "does not consist mainly in inventing new licks, but in stringing together learned licks and references in new and appropriate combinations."[17]

Jazz historians provide many confirmations of the idea that previously learned material plays a central role in improvisation. Observing that improvisers must develop great familiarity with "the (roughly) dozen chord types that most jazz improvising is based on," James Lincoln Collier indicates that most jazz is rooted in a basic "vocabulary" rather than an "anything goes" boundlessness; he also describes the typical improviser's mind as being "stuffed with a congeries of motifs, instrumental sounds, tiny figures, large structures, scales, chords, modes, and the rest of it," from which the player "works through association."[18] More specifically, Thomas Owens states that alto saxophonist Charlie Parker resembled "all important improvisers" when he "developed a personal repertory of melodic formulas that he used in the course of improvising," leading to the conclusion that "his 'spontaneous' performances were actually precomposed in part. This preparation was absolutely necessary, for no one can create fluent, coherent melodies in real time without having a well-rehearsed bag of melodic tricks ready."[19] Owens adds that Parker's formulas may be placed into several categories: occurring most frequently are figures only a few notes long and those with a variety of pitches, while the "complete phrases with well-defined harmonic implications" are encountered less often. The fact that the formulations of such a prodigious improviser can be so categorized provides further evidence that preparation and precomposition are mainstays of improvisatory jazz.

Asserting that Parker was "undoubtedly" the "greatest formulaic improviser" in jazz history, *The New Grove Dictionary of Jazz* notes moreover that formulaic improvisation itself is not limited to bebop but is "the most common kind of improvisation in jazz, spanning all styles."[20] Add such other varieties as paraphrase improvisation, motivic improvisation, and modal improvisation—whose very names point to types of raw material upon which variation, development, and construction may occur—and it becomes clear that jazz improvisation in general is firmly imbricated with practices based less on rigorously spontaneous invention than on the inspired elaboration of preexisting music material, notwithstanding the frequency with which a rhetoric of extemporaneous purity has been applied to it.

Spontaneous Writing

Returning to improvisatory literature, I have noted how strongly Kerouac's ideal of spontaneous composition was influenced by his perception of bop music, which he viewed in terms similar to those embraced by drummer Max Roach, who linked jazz innovation with modernity by saying, "We kept reading about rockets and jets and radar, and you can't play 4/4 music in times like that."[21] Kerouac decided that conventional prose was equally incongruous in such times and turned to writing "excitedly, swiftly, with writing-or-typing-cramps, in accordance . . . with laws of orgasm."[22]

As with the reascendance of jazz improvisation in the years after World War II, we may see Kerouac's change to a new writing style—carried out during the same period—as an effort to restore an auratic quality that, he felt, had been diminished or even lost in the literature of the day. Tracing numerous factors that contributed to Kerouac's concept of spontaneity, literary critic James T. Jones finds that his method imitated or parodied "the culture in which it developed" in that its "torrent of words . . . effectively mimics 1950s overproduction."[23] If we connect Kerouac's parody of overproduction with another factor proposed by Jones as a motivation for spontaneous prose, "reaction against the rigid social mores of the developing suburban culture," we may discover that Kerouac is not so much mimicking capitalist methods as subverting them, using an important result of frenetic writing—its foreclosure of the time necessary to engage in self-censorship, evasiveness, or pomposity—to achieve levels of "100% personal honesty both psychic and social etc."[24] that constitute his equivalent of the Benjaminian aura.

Again as in the case of postwar jazz, albeit with a somewhat different set of motivating and modifying circumstances, the impulse to use spontaneity as a route to renewed auratic qualities may have led Kerouac and other Beat writers to find in improvisation more values of originality and individuality than their practices actually entailed. It was a frequently expressed Beat notion that various forms of spontaneous composition can produce what William S. Burroughs called "a new dimension [in] writing"[25] and what Ginsberg called "wild phrasing . . . abstract poetry of mind . . . long saxophone-like chorus lines . . . really a new poetry."[26] Still, examination of methodologies used in Beat writing indicates that its composition was not always as extemporaneous as it appeared. Burroughs affirmed that the "best writing seems to be done almost by accident" but immediately added that one "cannot *will* spontaneity" and asserted that until he helped introduce the cut-up and fold-in procedures, based on scrambling prose physically in order to disrupt conventional meaning, "writers . . . had no way to produce the accident of spontaneity."[27] These quotations imply that in Burroughs's view, the bop compositions of Kerouac and Ginsberg are not truly spontaneous since their flow is to some extent "willed" into existence. Burroughs also emphasized that his own cut-up spontaneity was not based on random or haphazard juxtaposition, since after cutting or folding a text (or combining texts using these techniques) he would rewrite the result until it carried some degree of identifiable sense. "One tries not to impose story plot or continuity artificially but you do have to compose the materials," he observed. "[Y]ou can't just dump down a jumble of notes and thoughts and considerations and expect people to read it." And again, "I've done writing that I thought was interesting, experimentally, but simply not readable."[28] He therefore subjected his "jumbles" of dissected prose to rearrangement and revision before expecting readers to grapple with them. While the texts Burroughs used for cutting and folding were frequently his own, some were preexisting materials appropriated from the world of popular or literary culture; thus Burroughs joins the list of improvisers practicing elaboration as well as the invention idealized by romanticized discourse.

One might expect Kerouac, the most enthusiastic Beat proponent of that discourse, to be the member of the group most immune to such impurities. How could they creep into the work of an author who once criticized Ginsberg for correcting even the typographical errors in a manuscript, calling this a form of revision and therefore a violation of the "first thought best thought" rule? Kerouac stands accountable on this score in at least three ways, however.

1. His stream-of-consciousness prose was inspired by what novelist Henry Miller called "the idiomatic lingo of his time." Miller writes, "He 'invented it,' people will say. . . . What they should say is: 'He *got* it.' He got it, he dug it, he put it down."[29] This description makes Kerouac sound almost like a journalist or anthropologist, not originating but rather chronicling the sociolinguistic tenor of the scene in which he lived and traveled.

2. In addition to his boplike stream-of-consciousness method, Kerouac was strongly committed to a method that he called "sketching," which was also meant to be spontaneous but entailed the different technique of viewing or imagining a subject and then sketching it with words just as a visual artist would sketch it with lines. This device is probably the motivation for such phrases in his essay "Belief & Technique for Modern Prose" as "In tranced fixation dreaming upon object before you," and "Dont think of words when you stop but to see picture better."[30] The two methods of "sketching" and jazzlike "blowing" are not entirely distinct from each other, and at times their rhetoric overlaps, as when Kerouac writes that "sketching language is undisturbed flow from the mind of personal secret idea-words, *blow-*

ing (as per jazz musician) on subject of image."[31] But the dynamic of verbal sketching is by Kerouac's own definition less spontaneous than that of the bop-inspired technique, since it involves holding an image in consciousness (whether or not it is also before the eye) for as long as the writer needs to capture it in words. This is clear from "Essentials of Spontaneous Prose," which begins, "The object is set before the mind, either in reality, as in sketching (before a landscape or teacup or old face) or is set in the memory wherein it becomes the sketching from memory of a definite image-object."[32] However rapid and fluid the writing process may be, it does not seem wholly extemporaneous if it is linked to a sustained mental image that influences its content, its direction, and its final form.

3. Memory played an overarching role in Kerouac's methodology by providing source material that he returned to again and again. Despite his insistence that revision is antithetical to immediacy, his habit of revisiting certain personalities, events, ideas, and attitudes that preoccupied him throughout his career may itself constitute a sort of revision, described by literature critic Regina Weinreich as "quite literally a repetition of seeing (as the writer's imagination and memory go back over the past to redefine it)." Weinreich observes that as Kerouac wrote, "the elements of past experience were revised in the act of being recorded." Particular versions of the past were also revised in later accounts, moreover, as when he conceived the novel *Visions of Cody* as a corrective to inaccurate impressions conveyed by *On the Road* because of changes demanded by the publisher; his desire to convey his perceptions as accurately as possible "forced [his] mind over the material again and forces the reader to recognize that by such repetition a stage of revision is already built into the supposedly 'spontaneous' prose."[33] Jones calls on Neal Cassady's idea of "prevision" when he speculates that Kerouac may have "revised in his head before he wrote," citing biographer Gerald Nicosia's suggestion that Kerouac would often participate eagerly in life activities while at the same time "virtually *writing* . . . *in*

his head, so that the actual process of putting words on paper was but a mechanical extension of the process."[34] There are instances when Kerouac uses virtually the same phrases in different works to evoke material that affected him deeply; his highly romanticized description of an African American neighborhood in a journal entry for August 1949, for example, contains many passages that are virtually identical to a section of *On the Road,* which was largely composed during his famous typing marathon in April 1951, almost a year and a half later.[35] This strongly suggests that Kerouac put key experiences through obsessive prerehearsals that must indeed have turned some of his writing sessions into mere extensions of an ongoing mental process.

These points indicate that while Kerouac's improvisational writing certainly reflects a sense of immediacy that may be compared with that of a successful bebop performance, discursive claims of radical spontaneity and "nowness" do not comport with the practices he employed in achieving his effects.

Movies

Improvisation faces unusually high barriers in the field of motion pictures, since cinema's costly nature encourages planning and preparation before expensive film is exposed by trained technicians using valuable equipment. This does not mean that improvisation is unknown in cinema, however. Some mainstream directors, such as Robert Altman and Mike Leigh, use improvisation as a tool for developing characters and performances before the cameras roll. Some avant-garde directors, such as Andy Warhol and Jack Smith, have used low-budget techniques to produce nonnarrative and seminarrative films that allow for wholly extemporaneous acting and camera work. At other points along the spectrum, John Cassavetes made his 1959 production *Shadows* with entirely improvised performances, then reshot most of it with a script developed from that material; and Francis Ford Coppola has planned a production of Kerouac's novel *On the Road* using inexpensive sixteen-millimeter technology that would allow Russell Banks's screenplay (itself calling for a multiplicity of voice types, film stocks, camera techniques, and so on) to be supplemented via improvisational acting methods.[36]

Members of France's innovative Nouvelle Vague group have also drawn upon improvisation in some of their productions. Jacques Rivette has used the practice extensively in such works as *Out One: Spectre* (1972) and *Céline et Julie vont en bateau* (1974), for example, calling upon his performers for primary creative contributions (inventing narrative events, character traits, and dialogue) as well as the secondary contributions (interpreting a previously written screenplay) that would normally be expected of them.

Jean-Luc Godard, believed by many critics to be the most influential member of the Nouvelle Vague, is probably the best-known European filmmaker to have maintained a complex relationship with improvisation throughout his career. This relationship began in 1959 when he directed *À bout de souffle,* his first feature film. "I had written the first scene . . . and for the rest I had a pile of notes for each scene," he stated in a 1962 description of the production process. Initially anxious about this situation, he subsequently decided that "instead of planning ahead, I shall invent at the last minute," a procedure that he labeled "last-minute focusing."[37] Much of the dialogue was written the evening before a given scene was shot, and the movie was photographed without sound so that Godard could call out to the performers with the words he wanted them to say, in a sort of directorial ventriloquism; their actual voices were dubbed in later.

Extending the practice of last-minute focusing, scenes for his 1960 drama *Le Petit soldat* were often written during the same day when they were to be filmed, and an important episode of this movie taking the form of an interview was completely improvised by actress Anna Karina in a filming session guided by Godard's longtime admiration for Jean Rouch, a French ethnographic filmmaker who has directed both documentary and narrative works using wholly improvisational methods. Godard's third feature, *Une Femme est une femme* (1961), differed from its predecessors in that it adhered closely to a prepared scenario and was filmed in a studio rather than in real locations; yet much of its dialogue was written as the performers applied their makeup immediately before filming began.[38]

These works set the pattern for what became a steady habit of Godard: allowing improvisational elements to play a strong role in his productions through last-minute screenwriting, extemporaneous performances, intuitive manipulation of film footage during the editing process, and various combinations of these practices. Like the Beat Generation writers, he has cited values of authenticity and uniqueness in justifying his methods. "I didn't know exactly what I was going to do," he said of his 1962 drama *Vivre sa vie,* sounding very much like a spontaneous bop novelist. "I prefer to look for something I don't know. . . . In fact I made the film right off the bat, as if carried along, like an article written at one go. . . . I was so sincere in my desire to make the film that between us [himself and Karina, again his lead actress] we brought it off." And again, "One feels that if one is sincere and honest and one is driven into a corner over doing something, the result will necessarily be sincere and honest."[39]

Like the musicians and writers discussed above, Godard has been motivated in his search for alternative practices by the wish to restore an auratic quality to the art form with which he is engaged. Although he accepts the mechanical reproducibility of motion pictures as a given, recognizing this as a defining characteristic of the medium, he believes that modern cinema has been overwhelmed by commercialization and commodification that derive from the film industry's insistence on mass distribution and indiscriminate marketing of its products. "The trouble in the West is that we are overfed aesthetically. . . . We consume things that are unnecessary artistically," he has said.[40] His cultivation of an improvisational aesthetic has been motivated in part by his desire to evade film-industrial norms, and thereby to reinvigorate what he perceives as the artistic and expressive possibilities of cinema. His rhetoric, like that of other artists cited earlier, often places a romanticized emphasis on notions of spontaneity, authenticity, and individuality as idealized passageways to aesthetic originality and uniqueness. In his 1967 film *La Chinoise, ou plutôt à la chinoise,* for example, his intention was "to rediscover the cinema, to begin again."[41]

Significantly, *La Chinoise* was produced at the beginning of a period in Godard's career when he attempted to bypass the norms of mainstream film altogether, stripping away conventional elements of narrative and performance and rejecting conventional networks of distribution and exhibition. "I think the movie is not a thing which is taken by the camera," he said with regard to *La Chinoise,* explaining that instead, "the movie is the reality of the movie moving from reality to the camera. It's between them."[42] This insertion of a dynamic (and ungraspable) gap between the film and its means of realization points to Godard's desire for a discourse of auratic cinema. The same wish motivates characteristic statements he has made on the topic of cinematic originality, such as "I want to be able to see what is not seen; I don't want to show again what I've already seen, which is what most movies do."[43] At his most radical, Godard attempts to divorce what he sees as the purity of cinema from the contamination of everyday language. "Today we live in an epoch of total power being given to all forms of rhetoric, a time of terrorism of language," he said in 1983, adding that he wishes "to speak of things before words and names take over" and to deal "with things that may soon no longer exist or . . . with things which do not exist yet."[44]

One means of accomplishing these goals is to film improvisational performances, which exist only on the spur of the ephemeral moment. Another is to extend the idea of improvisation into all phases of cinematic production; consider Godard's statement that extemporaneous invention "takes place in front of the movieola [editing machine] just as much as it does on the set."[45] Another is to resist the generally held distinction between fiction (narrative) and nonfiction (documentary) cinema, holding instead that all cinema is ultimately nonfiction since *(a)* photography always has an indexical relationship with reality[46] and *(b)* moving-image photography captures the mutability of reality in ways that even fictional frameworks cannot obscure. Still another is to replace the idea of "picture," represented by a fixed (objective) photograph, with that of "image," spontaneously created in the mind of the (subjective) observer. One statement of this principle occurs in Godard's quasi-autobiographical 1994 film *JLG/JLG—December Self-Portrait:* "An image is the creation of the mind by drawing together two different realities; the further apart the realities, the stronger the image."

Yet while the evolution of such notions may be traced through Godard's entire oeuvre, he has also recognized the limitations of spontaneity and improvisation in artistic work. As early as 1962, he contrasted his practice of "last-minute focusing" with the idea of improvisation per se, contending that "you can modify up to a point, but when shooting begins it should change as little as possible, otherwise it's catastrophic."[47] Various other statements have revealed how substantially his discursive embrace of contingency has been balanced by a pragmatic acknowledgment of the problems posed by cinematic improvisation. Answering a questioner who inquired about his "techniques of improvisation," he responded, "I make movies as though I'm living a day of my life. No one improvises their life—at least, I never have." When another questioner raised the issue of improvisation, he again rejected that term, subsequently linking it with "chance" and stating that when one employs chance, the results might be "good once and bad a hundred times. . . . I'd like to work both by chance and by control."[48]

Godard's explanations of his improvisational practices often recall Kerouac's methodologies. Kerouac's habitual use of a narrative framework to shape and contain extemporaneous invention prefigures Godard's remark, "It's only because I have a narrative line in mind that I'm able to improvise and to go on shooting every day." Kerouac's periodic return to particular ideas, interests, and characters is echoed by Godard's admission that "quite often when I make movies I discover that I'm making again, in a very different way, something I've done already."[49] Kerouac's habit of mentally prerehearsing material that he would later commit to paper finds a reflection in Godard's comment that he makes improvisatory use only of "material which goes a long way back. Over the years you accumulate things and then suddenly you use them in what you're doing."[50] Each similarity of approach between Godard and Kerouac underscores the manner in which the ideal of extemporaneous creation is tempered in practice by realities of repetition, preconceptualization, and control, all of which are found in jazz improvisation as well.

Gibberish Versus Control

Kerouac addresses a root issue of improvisatory prose in his novel *Desolation Angels,* initially completed in 1956 and published in 1965, when he depicts a conversation between Jack Duluoz, the character standing in for himself, and another man representing poet Randall Jarrell, whom Kerouac admired.[51]

"How can you get any refined or well gestated thoughts into a spontaneous flow as you call it? It can all end up gibberish," says the Jarrell figure, leading the Kerouac figure to reply, "If it's gibberish, it's gibberish. There's a certain amount of control going on like a man telling a story in a bar without interruptions or even one pause." This response indicates Kerouac's clear awareness of the "spontaneous" writer as a deliberative artist whose speed and fluency must not be mistaken for heedlessness, carelessness, or a lack of coherent goals and efficacious techniques. Like improvisers in the neighboring fields of music and cinema, he balances an idealized rhetoric of auratic authenticity and individuality with a judicious use of preexisting aesthetic frameworks and "previsioned" artistic materials. While his employment of such frameworks and materials may amount to a demystification of improvisational "purity," the freshness of his results and the energy of his procedures reconfirm the ideal of extemporaneous creation as a firmly grounded instrumentality for specific types of artistic production.

CONSTRUCTING THE GROTESQUE BODY IN WORD, IMAGE, AND SOUND

> The grotesque image reflects a phenomenon in transformation. . . . The relation to time is one determining trait of the grotesque image.
>
> —Bakhtin, *Rabelais and His World*

Discussing the multifarious nature of grotesquerie in art and culture, literary theorist Mikhail Bakhtin notes that the grotesque body "is not a closed, completed unit; it . . . transgresses its own limits."[1] The realms of film and sound recording are populated by nothing but grotesque bodies, with polymorphous possibilities set free by their very disconnection from the physical world. In cinema, bodies are deprived of solidity and three-dimensionality; in audiophony, they are bereft of visibility and attachment to a material source; in both, they are susceptible to the many covert and overt manipulations that are customarily the lot of constructions, assemblages, and representations.

This essay is an excursion into the world of cinematic and audiophonic freakishness, focusing on a handful of radically innovative works that share an impulse to reconstruct and reconfigure our fundamental notions of what the body is, what we think the body is, and what the body might become if conventional notions of its meanings and implications were interrogated and overturned. The books, films, and recordings that I examine differ from each other as much as they diverge from more time-honored currents of Western aesthetics, but all partake of the semiotics-scrambling spirit represented most fulsomely in the Beat tradition by William S. Burroughs, the great granddaddy of drastic prose. "Nobody is permitted to leave the biologic theater," he writes in *Nova Express,* but that prohibition never stopped him—or the limited number of modernist and postmodernist artists with similarly exorbitant imaginations—from trying.

Decapitations

The protean filmmaker Raul Ruiz has noted that cinema commonly presents its spectators with "a series of decapitations," in which cuts from wide shots to close-ups (or from one close-up to another) amount to bodily amputations. Cinema is thus a community of freaks and monsters with "hyper-realist . . . excessive" characteristics; if we fail to notice these in our everyday moviegoing experiences, it is because the mechanisms of classical film style (narrative continuity, "invisible" editing, the matching of sound with image, and so on) are designed to camouflage their most conspicuous traits by means of arbitrary conventions that we are trained from childhood to comprehend and accept.[2] The privileged place of such grotesquerie in media representation is emblematic of the material body's psychically driven tendency to transgress its limits in phantasmic terms. Ruiz is among the few narrative filmmakers to take account of this in both theory and practice. When a femme fatale does a striptease in his film *Three Crowns for the Sailor,* as Ethan Spigland notes, the protagonist "is horrified to discover that her nipples and vulva are only prostheses, and that her mouth is her only orifice. Nudity is impossible in Ruiz's world because the body of an actor is already a fiction, a simulacrum."[3] The body stripped bare is just another trompe l'oeil, another "trap or . . . puzzle" indicating the ultimate instability of not only cinema but the world that it represents.[4]

To be sure, the body need not be visually represented in order to manifest the grotesque. It may be constructed through words or sounds, which may themselves be assembled and inflected in ways influenced by cinematic techniques. Literary works written in a wide range of traditional styles aim for the transparency of meaning that has come to dominate classical film. Others, including many by the Beat Generation writers, do not. No member of the core Beat group was more adventurous in this regard than Burroughs, the most prominent champion of the cut-up and fold-in methods, which call for the writer to cut or fold a preexisting text and use this as the basis for a new work (the cut-up or fold-in can be either rewritten or presented as is) marked by chance and randomness. Bodies of text created in such ways are acts of trompe l'oeil on the printed page, appearing as ordinary blocks of prose until reading reveals them as expansive networks of faux continuity, discontinuity, and paracontinuity that explode conventional ideals of linearity and coherence.

In principle, the cut-up and fold-in have clear parallels with cinematic montage, which similarly involves the elision and recombination of semiotic material, and effects in Burroughs's writing have been duly likened to effects of cinema. Burroughs himself found the results of fold-in composition to be "analogous to the flashback in film," and critic John Tytell has attributed the entropic fastidiousness of Burroughs's literary vision to his presentation of "precise, clinically observed and unemotionally rendered details . . . presented cinematically, with all the speed of the motion-picture lens."[5] Some of Burroughs's novels (e.g., *Junkie, Queer*) exploit selected conventions of linear narrative, but his greatest contributions to modernist-postmodernist literature have taken bold avant-garde routes. Cinematic variants of the cut-up method have also been used successfully in avant-garde film, most notably in Antony Balch's films (*Towers Open Fire* [1963], *The Cut-Ups* [1966]) with Burroughs as actor or narrator or both.

More broadly, Burroughs's innovative compositional systems have an interesting relationship with issues of longstanding importance in film theory. A key point of origin for Burroughs's cut-up aesthetic is his desire to forge a stance of purposeful irrationality as a means of attacking the manifold ills of twentieth-century culture that he metaphorically represents through the visions of cosmic conspiracy that underlie his personal mythology. His work suggests that, in critic Gregory Stephenson's words, "language is a system that carries implicit patterns of perception and thought that are largely unconscious in the user of the language; these patterns are the assumptions of the system; and all patterns, all systems are reductive."[6] As a purveyor of denotative and connotative meanings with characteristics similar to (although not identical with) those of verbal language,[7] film becomes in Burroughs's view "a metaphor for total control, a 'reality studio' which must be challenged and subverted" by disrupting habitual patterns of understanding and placing signifiers (words, images, and combinations thereof) into subversive new contexts.[8]

The archvillain of Burroughs's mythology, the doubly named Mr. Bradly Mr. Martin, has as his agents "all the authorities and all the establishments and all the systems . . . anyone in a position to impose and enforce a reality on another," in Stephenson's concise description.[9] This recalls the argument of philosopher Louis Althusser that self-empowered authorities, establishments, and systems have consolidated the power to reproduce themselves and their effects by seizing the attention of individuals (*interpellating* is Althusser's term for this) through what he calls Ideological State Apparatuses, social institutions that seduce the inherently fragmented self with the illusion of monadic coherence, upon which further illusions may be built for the benefit of the entrenched power system, whatever social, political, and economic shape this may happen to take.[10]

Burroughs's defense against interpellation is a radical montage based on discontinuity, non sequitur, irrelevance, and the sort of "systematic derangement of the senses" that poet Arthur Rimbaud famously advocated. Burroughs warns that "all association tracks are obsessional" and advises that "irrelevant response" is effective in breaking out of them.[11] Even seemingly self-evident concepts like one's own existence as "body" and "animal" are mere "verbal labels," he declares.[12] Hence his loyalty to the cut-up and fold-in methods, which unhinge and discombobulate the language realities promulgated by entrenched sociocultural enemies of all kinds, represented by the reality-scripting Nova Mob in his literary mythos. He encourages us to replace our internalized self-images with flamboyant "verbal bodies" whose grotesquerie flies beyond ingrained conceptions of our material and psychological world.

Burroughs's proudly paranoid vision of existence, in which Tytell finds "distortions of the body and spirit [that] create a spectacle of suffering in the Dadaist and Surrealist tradition," recalls Antonin Artaud's pursuit of a Theater of Cruelty that anticipated key elements of Burroughs's ethos.[13] In this atmosphere, Edward Halsey Foster notes, *disorientation* is "the way out of the fixation that language has on the mind. Fighting his enemies on their own ground, Burroughs creates greater conflicts than they do. . . . [H]e dissolves the expectations and certainties of semantic order, thereby leaving members of the Nova Mob mumbling nonsense."[14] The cut or folded text, film, and body are Burroughs's favored means of release from "the discreteness, the exclusiveness of an either/or universe into a multivalent infinity where all sets intersect," as Stephenson writes. "By cutting the word lines we can restructure our reality, our consciousness."[15]

T,O,U,C,H,I,N,G Zorns Lemma

Many avant-garde filmmakers have aimed to reconfigure entrenched conceptions of reality by overturning the linear mindsets of conventional communication. Such major figures as Stan

Brakhage, Jack Smith, Harry Smith, Michael Snow, and Kenneth Anger come readily to mind, all approaching this project from very different perspectives and with very different methodologies. The films I have selected for analysis here—*T,O,U,C,H,I,N,G* by Paul Sharits (1968) and *Zorns Lemma* by Hollis Frampton (1970)—diverge from each other in important ways, but they share a deep fascination with the need to rethink both verbal and cinematic language, arriving in this process at innovative paradigms for the "body" of the cinematic text.

The goals of the films are suggested by their titles. *T,O,U,C,H,I,N,G* breaks an everyday word into a series of individual letters, recalling the ambition of the Lettrist movement—one of Sharits's great precursors in avant-garde art—to free the unique expressive presence of the letter from the tyranny of the larger discursive units (the phrase, the sentence, and so on) that bind it. *Zorns Lemma* invokes a name (Zorn) and a term *(lemma)* relating to a specialized field (mathematical set theory) that is unfamiliar to most outsiders, thereby asking spectators to make a cognitive and imaginative leap before the film has even started to unspool.

A key strategy of both films is to sever two kinds of semiotic continuity—the seductive flow of integrated narrative, and the one-to-one matching of word and image—that conventional movies use to divert attention from cinema's inherently fragmented nature and construct the sort of seamless audiovisual discourse that audiences have been trained to find aesthetically unified and psychologically alluring. The purposefully disruptive tactics of these films (and filmmakers) have much in common with those of Burroughs in his most radically inventive prose. More specifically, these works find Sharits and Frampton exploring the dialectics of word and image in a spirit similar to that with which Burroughs probed dialectical relationships between the materiality of verbal language and the galaxies of coercive meaning attached thereto by the cultural, sociopolitical, and psychological power structures he feared and loathed.

Zorns Lemma and *T,O,U,C,H,I,N,G* are creatively concerned with two kinds of dialectical relationship: (1) the overarching dialectic between filmic-photographic imagery and written-spoken language, and (2) the dialectic within each of those two-part categories—between cinematic shot and photographic image, on one hand, and between written language and spoken language, on the other. Each thus functions in its own way as a radical critique of film-as-language and of language-as-film.

The films have other similarities, as well. They are both interested in "mentalizing . . . the space of film," in Rosalind Krauss's words.[16] They are both concerned with the dialectical juxtaposition of two-dimensional and three-dimensional fields.[17] And each takes the broadest of the dialectics mentioned above (that between image and language) in directions that privilege visual experience over auditory experience. *T,O,U,C,H,I,N,G* does this by transforming vocal speech into a noiselike musique concrète that operates in counterpoint to the image track—which consists of similarly reified bursts of color and imagery—instead of obeying the communicative logic that ordinarily governs the spoken word, in cinema as in life. *Zorns Lemma* begins with language in a state of relative clarity (and predominance over the image) but ends with language in a state of relative obscurity (and parity with the image), with a period of richly construed ambivalence between these two phases. Details of these trajectories will be discussed below.

Both of the works discussed here fit the category of avant-garde cinema called Structural Film, a label devised by film historian P. Adams Sitney to designate works characterized by fixed camera position, flicker effect (exploiting the stroboscopic impact of contrasting frames edited in rapid alternation), loop (repetitive) printing, and/or rephotography from the screen. *T,O,U,C,H,I,N,G* has all these ingredients, while *Zorns Lemma* has a few instances of rephotography and makes brilliant use of fixed camera position during its culminating section. Both incorporate some of the additional traits that critic Malcolm Le Grice cites in his account of Structural Film, including a concern with the semantics of the image and a desire to use duration as a concrete dimension of the work.[18] More generally, each film uses elements of cinematic structure as part of its actual content—most notably, characteristics of film stock and photographic procedure in the Sharits and ludic juxtaposition of semantically disjunctive images in the Frampton.

David E. James usefully traces the evolution or "modulation" of structural film during its heyday, from an early phase when it has an analogous relationship with minimal art (an insistence on materiality, a quest for "clarified rational" configurations) to a later phase when it has more concern with "conceptual activities" that call into question "disjunctions and identities" relating to the nature, creation, and reception of an artistic work. From this modulation arises "a general subordination of interest in representation, especially of narrative"; a new stress on medium-specific materials, resources, conditions, and significations; and a "generalized assumption" that the necessary condition for Structural Film is a concern "with materials as language and with language as material." A similar evolution can be found in Burroughs's work, from its early engagement with the terse prose styles of American pulp fiction to its later experimentation with materialist methodologies and the subordination of linear narrative. We move away from Burroughs's aesthetic when we note James's argument that the overall nature of Structural Film leads toward a tautological situation whereby the success of a work lies in the fulfillment of predetermined operational procedures—a fulfillment that may be merely mechanical or perfunctory—since Burroughs uses his predetermined procedures not in a rigorously unswerving manner but as aids in reaching artistic results that have strong currents of intuitive flexibility and personal expressiveness woven into their bizarre fabrics. We can detect parallels with Burroughs again, however, when James defends such Structural films by arguing that "any impulse toward . . . a scientism . . . is re-contained as itself one element in a field of mutually ironizing processes" that fend off the scientific even as they incorporate it. Structural Film thus emerges as a cinematic analogue of the New Criticism in literature, dominated by irony and by the reliance of irony on "thrust and counterthrust" as a primary source of semiotic stability.[19] If internal tension is indeed a key element of Structural Film, then Structural Film is a privileged arena for analyzing and exploring dialectical relationships between counterpoised cinematic elements, including image and language. Such investigations take exceptionally revealing forms in the Sharits and Frampton works that I am discussing here, as they do in the literary works by Burroughs that explore related concerns.

Sharits

Throughout his career, Sharits has found great resonance in Structural Film's dialectical possibilities. *T,O,U,C,H,I,N,G* is one of his most powerful works, providing an especially vigorous example of his interest in "the differences between sound and visual image" and his distaste for "associative relations between sight and sound—for instance where sounds create images or where an image is obviously the source of its sound."[20] The film as a whole is a concentrated stream of rapidly changing frames—some presenting fields of pure color, others depicting letters (those of the title word) or images—accompanied by similarly elusive sounds.

Although it is the last of Sharits's flicker films, *T,O,U,C,H,I,N,G* is not a pure exercise in that form, since it plays its colored "empty" frames against images that take on a narrative quality by virtue of their incremental development. In addition to these quasi-narrative sequences, there is another sequential "event" within the film as well, conveyed through images of eye surgery and a sexual act; but this is presented in a manner so elliptical and nonlinear that it seems intended less as an incident to be understood than as a string of arbitrary mood-inducing signifiers.[21]

One of the film's seminarrative sequences consists of still-photo shots picturing a man (played by David Franks, a poet) in two poses: with a pair of scissors held to his outthrust tongue and with a woman's long fingernails poised menacingly over his face. During the first portions of the film, the scissors maintain their apparent threat while the fingernails take on a closer and even more aggressive position; eventually all of the sharp objects retreat from the frame, however, and the man is ultimately seen (now with his eyes open) apparently protruding from the frame while, in Sharits's description, "the screen appears to collapse, in rhythmic pulses, into itself."[22]

The other seminarrative sequence (often overlooked in descriptions of the film) is the appearance of the eight letters of the title, one at a time, over the course of the work. The word's incremental arrival obviously echoes the comma-ridden orthography of the film's title; together these displays of the printed word recall the Lettrist project of deploying linguistic particles in such a way that "immediate meaning" is eradicated and, in Greil Marcus's words, each element exists only *"in so far as it allows one to imagine another element which is either nonexistent or possible."*[23] (Sharits's use of this quasi-Derridean strategy is consistent with his tendency as a writer to construct highly physicalized prose that verges at times on concrete poetry.[24]) There is another overtly linguistic component in the film, moreover: on the sound track, Franks speaks the word *destroy.* At first this sounds like a repetitive loop recording. The sound of the word gradually changes, however, shifting its phonemes in subtle but noticeable ways that render the sound not *un*intelligible but *ambiguously* intelligible, leading different listeners to "understand" different meanings as the film proceeds.[25]

Sharits's treatment of the printed word in *T,O,U,C,H,I,N,G* is integral to his treatment of cinematic form, which persistently breaks visual elements apart, the better to perceive and appreciate their discrete qualities and characteristics. Color is experienced not only as the coloration of objects but also as pure color fields; images appear as if wrenched from conventional meaning-sequences and momentarily frozen in time; the shape of the frame is emphasized by its varying relationship with elements placed inside it; and the film as a whole is divided into segments as distinct and mutually balanced as the letters of the title. Like many other Sharits works, *T,O,U,C,H,I,N,G* is an intensely analytic experience. One function of its alternations between filmed image and printed word is to literalize *cutting* as the work's dominant and dominating trope; although neither the scissors nor the fingernails do the damage they threaten—this is a clear mark of the film's sixties-pacifist political thrust—the work revels in hyperbolic dissections of its celluloid, graphic, and semiotic components. Nothing could be more in keeping with Burroughs's cut-up aesthetic, and Sharits has duly acknowledged his fascination with it.[26]

The film's treatment of the spoken word takes a different but closely related form. The single oral utterance of the film ("destroy") is given a great deal of *near*-repetition that echoes the image track's variation-within-sameness. Yet unlike the frames containing letters and pictures, which retain their recognizable contents, and unlike the color frames, which retain their various hues, the word is altered to the point where its phonologic properties cross the line of recognizability and their original signification is lost.[27] It has been suggested that repetition alone is responsible for this seeming loss or change of signification,[28] and Sharits has written (drawing on Edgar Allan Poe) that "'[t]o repeat, monotonously, some common word, until the sound . . . ceased to convey any idea to the mind, to lose all sense of motion or physical existence' *is* a major (ir)rationale of the soundtracks" of both *T,O,U,C,H,I,N,G* and *S:TREAM:S:S:ECTION:-S:ECTION:S:S:ECTIONED*, his next film.[29] Still, close attention to the *T,O,U,C,H,I,N,G* sound track confirms that the word-loop does undergo a gradual alteration that materially changes its sound. In any case, the *effect* is of the phonemes being rearranged in some way—not the "invisible" way of a classical film-editing or sound-editing splice but a deliberately detectable way also exemplified by the plainly visible "dam splices" of

S:S:S:S:S:S. (Cinematic splices are normally placed between frames, but in that work—which shows water flowing in a rural stream—horizontal splice-bars bisect certain frames, punctuating and interrupting the movie's otherwise steady flow and providing one of its most expressive elements. Cornwell accurately describes them as "film analogues to the images of rocks and boulders which appear on the screen."[30])

The printed word in *T,O,U,C,H,I,N,G* has an inherent verbal quality that gives it a built-in dialectical relation to such nonverbal elements as the color fields and iconic frames; at the same time, its letter-by-letter appearance is of a piece with the overall visual structure of the film, which operates as a series of bursts or explosions. The film's printed-word component therefore serves a dual function, dialectical from one perspective and analogous from another.[31] By contrast, the insistent near-repetitions of the spoken word have a primarily dialectical relationship with the visuals accompanying them; their steadiness and consistency contrast with the plosive irruptions of imagery, just as in *S:S:S:S:S:S* the intrusive horizontality of the "dam splices" contrasts with the flowing verticality of the scratches made by Sharits on the film emulsion and with the flowing illusionism of the stream that is the film's ostensible subject.

If the Lettrist project of Isidore Isou was to "rescue the letter from the word,"[32] the audiovisual project of Sharits has been (far more sensibly) to rescue the specifically *filmic* from the diffusely *cinematic.*[33] Immediately after *T,O,U,C,H,I,N,G* was completed, this project led him to try removing from his work all traces of "literary structures and dramatic-psychological themes," along with "influences of painting" and "senses of emotionality" evoked or produced by color rhythms.[34] The first result was the brilliant *S:S:S:S:S:S,* followed by works whose very titles signal an ever-growing fascination with the filmic for its own sake, for example, *Analytical Studies II: Un-Framed Lines* (1971–76), *Color Sound Frames* (1974), and *Apparent Motion* (1975).[35]

Frampton

Frampton also zeroes in on specific properties of film for its own sake, using a different set of methods and techniques. Arguing that *cinema* is a Greek word meaning *movie,* he rejects the "assumption" that film frames must be configured so as to sustain the illusion of movement; citing the "structural logic of the filmstrip," he proposes to "call our art simply: film."[36] Frampton's approach to this "structural logic" has been enormously varied, but never has it been more stimulating than in *Zorns Lemma,* which exhibits (among many other things) a vivid engagement with the possibilities of irony[37] and a keen sense of the riches to be gleaned from exploring the dialectics of image and language—a sense also found in other Frampton works, including such masterpieces as *Poetic Justice* (1971) and *(nostalgia)* (1972), the first two sections of his ambitious *Hapax Legomena* series.

Zorns Lemma counterpoints image and language in three fundamental ways. During the first portion, the screen is entirely blank, but the sound track is active with a recitation from the *Bay State Primer,* an instructional book published in 1800. The long second portion reverses this configuration, eliminating the sound track and filling the screen with two sorts of imagery: motionless shots focusing on printed words (commercial signs, public notices, etc.) and, replacing these images one at a time, moving image shots depicting gestures, movements, and activi ties (walking, painting, changing a car tire, etc.). The third portion resolves the sound-picture disparity by offering both sound and image tracks but with a twist: the spoken words are mechanically chanted to the beat of a ticking metronome, and the image (a lengthy shot of people crossing a snow-covered field) becomes increasingly attenuated, ultimately fading into whited-out obscurity as the aperture of Frampton's camera is gradually opened to its maximum exposure level.

The film's most obvious ordering principles are those of the alphabet and the clock. The opening *Bay State Primer* recitation is drawn from an alphabetically arranged text ("In *Adam's* fall we sinned all/Thy life to mend God's *book* attend," and so forth). Also alphabetical are the initial letters of the printed words in the film's central section; furthermore, the replacement of word-containing images with nonword shots proceeds according to the (inverse) frequency of each initial letter's occurrence in the English-language vocabulary.[38] Meanwhile, each of the shots in this section occupies twenty-four frames of film and is therefore one second long.[39] In addition, the metronomic spoken words of the third section are timed to occur at one-second intervals, thereby measuring (loosely) the length of the eleventh-century text they come from and (accurately) the duration of the imagery on the screen.

The dialectic of image and language thus operates in two ways within the film. One way is contrapuntal, as when printed words appear within images during part 2 and when an arbitrarily fragmented reading accompanies a continuous flow of imagery in part 3. The other is sequential, as when image-absence and sonic-presence in part 1 give way to image-presence and sonic-absence in part 2 and thence to image-presence and sonic-presence in part 3; and when linguistic signifiers are replaced (albeit intermittently) by nonlinguistic signifiers during the course of part 2.

James has discussed *Zorns Lemma* in productive ways, and some of his points regarding the language-image dialectic are useful here.[40] He observes that while the *Bay State Primer* passage used in part 1 proposes objects (nouns) as "dominant ordering elements," the passage's rhetoric does not emphasize the value of words as "the nomenclature for preexistent things" but simply as linguistic elements calculated to produce a correct linguistic order of a particular type, governed by various formal parameters including alphabetical positioning. Part 2 then applies an alphabetical taxonomy to the world as represented in film, but this leads to the (ironic) result that nonverbal imagery and the material presence of film itself progressively subvert the hegemony of language. Making sense of the film's verbal content calls for procedures quite different from those used in reading printed texts, moreover, so tensions arise between verbal and nonverbal apprehension, partly because of the film's own (ironically) pedagogical function. Ultimately alphabetical control fails—even as language refuses to be excluded—and "the terms of an autonomous filmic grammar appear." The film's last section juxtaposes an emerging "oblivion of complete light" with a text that is about light and which echoes the image track by losing its "ability to mean" through being recited in a metronomic way that disrupts its linear flow. (Frampton clearly resembles Burroughs in his fascination with language that discards its ability to mean, notwithstanding the divergent paths they take in exploring this.)

What needs more attention is the full implication of the dissolution of the final section's spoken text—from *On Light, or the Ingression of Forms* by Robert Grosseteste—into "abstract sound," as James describes it. Turning back to the *Bay State Primer* text in the film's first section, even this has something of an "abstract" character, since it is shaped as much by formal (alphabetical) determinants as by a desire to convey meaning. Hence it reminds us that, in music theorist Jean-Jacques Nattiez's words, a "proliferation of *formal* interpretants is . . . characteristic of symbolic phenomena basic to domains otherwise saturated with the indisputable presence of 'signifieds,' domains such as literature or discursive thought." By way of example, Nattiez continues, "Do not the rhymes at the end of a line of verse depend on symbolic functioning of a musical type? Is it truly for the sake of their meaning alone that one opposes the phrases 'the theory of practice and the practice of theory' (Bourdieu) or 'the poetry of grammar and the grammar of poetry' (Jakobson)? It is interesting to look at the functioning of our so-called 'associations of *ideas*,' which are more often than not dictated by assonance or purely phonetic or rhythmic connections."[41] Such connections work to materialize utterance, foregrounding the sensory and submerging the significatory.

The film's treatment of the Grosseteste passage in its last section carries this further. The text speaks of light while light engulfs the film. Yet the words cannot speak effectively in the ways that Grosseteste intended, since Frampton subjects them to a formal operation that profoundly transforms them. If in *Poetic Justice* the filmmaker "attempts the impossible sublimation of the figural into the textual within cinema,"[42] here he attempts the desublimation of the textual into the material, that is, into the word-as-noise and the image-as-photon. This is accomplished by the growing flood of light, which ultimately absorbs all image, and by the insistent metronome, which strikes each word as unfailingly as a drumbeat punctuates the "destroy"-destroying loop of *T,O,U,C,H,I,N,G*—another film that draws image out of itself and leads speech away from meaning, toward the rarefied domain of musication that fascinated Artaud, and toward glossolalia, described by Allen S. Weiss as "the enunciation of a pure signifier—the refusal of meaning and the valorization of pure voice," in which "it is the body that speaks."[43]

The full language-image dialectic of both films therefore lies not only in the relation of language and image to each other but in the relation of both to the materiality in which they are rooted, much as Burroughs's cut and folded texts explore dialogic tensions between words as carriers of meaning and words as physical objects in the world. Word becomes noise as image merges into light (Frampton) or struggles to escape the frame (Sharits). In the process, desublimation yields a paradoxical sublimity.

Soundbodies

> Sometimes sounds that have no real meaning mean more to us.
>
> —Robert Wilson in Lawrence Shyer, *Robert Wilson and His Collaborators*

> Language is a whore.
>
> —William S. Burroughs in Lawrence Shyer, *Robert Wilson and His Collaborators*

When he allows his physical voice to be incarnated by recording techniques, Burroughs puts more trust in linear construction and conventional communication patterns than one finds in much of his printed work. The text he recites may have been created through the cut-up or fold-in method, but the recitation itself generally proceeds from beginning to middle to end, like a poetry reading in the classic Beat sense. The most aurally stimulating events in his recordings tend to emerge from the voluptuous care with which he pronounces a favored (often mystically tinged) syllable[44] or the playfulness with which he lets go of decorum and engages in ludic revelation of some particularly ironic intersection between a chosen text and his own performative personality.[45] Broadly speaking, the possibilities of building grotesque bodies in sound have been more systematically and thoroughly pursued by audio artists (e.g., Gregory Whitehead) and by composers who use the spoken voice as a malleable raw material to be manipulated and restructured via technological procedures. Whether or not they acknowledge a debt to Burroughs—debt of a kind suggested by the paired quotations above—their innovations and explorations often move down modernist and postmodernist pathways that he played a key role in discovering and revealing.

A striking example of grotesque-body construction via recorded words is *I Am Sitting in a Room*, a 1970 work by composer Alvin Lucier that has been realized more than once in different venues.[46] It begins with the performer reciting a brief text (stating the procedures and intentions of the work itself) into a tape recorder. The recording is then played back—not through output-input cables but through the ambient space of the performance room—into a second tape recorder. *This* recording is then played back to the first recorder, and then *that* tape is re-recorded by the second recorder, and so on. This re-re-recording process is repeated a predetermined number of times until several generations have been completed, and these recordings—from the first to the last, heard in sequential order—constitute the completed work.[47]

The first generation sounds like ordinary recorded speech. The second is similar, but a distinct echo effect is noticeable. Subsequent generations sound less and less like speech, eventually turning into musique concrète shaped so completely by electronic means that the original source of the sound (the voice of a human performer) would be impossible to determine for a listener who had not heard the early portions of the piece. The continuous change in the nature of the sound gives the work a "narrative" structure, as the performer's voice (implying the performer's physical body) gradually loses ground to the sonic characteristics of the room where the recordings were made and to the increasingly conspicuous imprecision of the electronic techniques and devices used to make them. "Those sounds common to the original spoken statement and those implied by the structural dimensions of the room are reinforced and grow louder," as Lucier puts it in the annotations to his record-album version of the piece, while "the others are gradually eliminated."[48] The resulting work is not a record of a biological body's voice but a record of the construction of a composite "body" comprising corporeal, architectural, and technological elements. This is a superbly ambiguous monstrosity, to be sure—and one that refuses to relinquish its dialogic open-endedness in space and time, since it is capable of being re-created in a near-infinite number of circumstances by a near-endless number of performers, and with near-infinite flexibility as to the number of sound generations through which it is carried.

A more aggressive approach—and one more resonant with Burroughs's cut-up aesthetic—is found in Steve Reich's early pieces for recorded voice. *It's Gonna Rain,* composed in 1965, uses as source material the voice of an African American street preacher recorded (along with traffic and other ambient noises) in an outdoor urban location. Divided into two sections, the piece begins with two identical tape loops playing in unison, then moving gradually out of phase with each other, then back to unison. The second portion uses longer loops that similarly slide out of phase and are then joined by two more loops out of phase with the first pair. The piece concludes with an eight-voice sequence that Reich describes as "a kind of controlled chaos, which may be appropriate to the subject matter—the end of the world."[49] As in the Lucier piece, the owner of the recorded voice begins the work as an implied biological body, but when the sound is profoundly transformed—to the extent that it becomes hard to identify as human—it acquires a new "identity" as rhythm and melody take precedence over sense and semiosis.

The eschatological interests of *It's Gonna Rain* give way to more directly political concerns in *Come Out*, composed and realized by Reich in 1966.[50] Here the source material is the voice of a nineteen-year-old man describing a beating he has received in a Harlem police station. This work again capitalizes on Reich's realization that melody and rhythm occur naturally in speech and become enhanced when they are underscored through the simple repetition of brief samples. *Come Out* begins with a comparatively long spoken phrase, then isolates a small portion and draws out its inherent melodic and rhythmic qualities by repeating it several times; then Reich's "phasing" process takes over, first giving the sound a gradually increasing reverberation effect, and then giving it canonic form by multiplying it into two, four, and finally eight concurrent lines. In this way Reich builds an artificial and polyphonic (dialogic) artifact out of a spontaneously occurring and unitary (monologic) source.

After showing keen interest in tape-recorded voices during the early years of his career, Reich started putting most of his energy into music for conventional (and unconventional) instruments, turning temporarily away from the more technologically inclined side of his talent. (The ambitious *My Name Is*, a late-seventies work involving technological manipulations of multiple voices, is an exception.) When he returned to this arena in the late 1980s, it was in a very different context, using brief voice samples as wholly integrated elements in what is otherwise an instrumental piece. *Different Trains* finds Reich again choosing source material with complex cultural implications, including words spoken by Holocaust survivors and a retired railroad worker. All are relevant to his project, which is to craft a historically and politically evocative dialogue between reminiscences of his own childhood train journeys in the United States and evocations of simultaneous journeys made by people (most notably Holocaust victims) in vastly different circumstances. The speech-related component of the work was generated through a six-part process: recording spoken words and phrases; choosing appropriate fragments of the recorded material; enhancing the melodic and rhythmic characteristics of these fragments by isolating and repeating them; notating these melodies and rhythms in standard music-writing form so that musical instruments will be able to imitate and accompany them; blending the voice tapes (by means of a computer and sampling keyboards) with similarly manipulated train sounds; and using the resulting composite tape—a constructed "body" that incorporates the implied "bodies" of the speakers whose voices are heard—as the fifth "member" of an ensemble that is in other respects a conventional string quartet.[51]

A similar but more carnivalesque approach is taken by Scott Johnson in *John Somebody* and *No Memory,* both recorded in 1986.[52] Each section of *John Somebody* begins with a previously recorded vocal phrase that contains (approximately) the specific pitches and rhythms with which Johnson wants to work. He edits these to bring out the particular musical values he finds most attractive, and then loops, layers, and mixes them on a multitrack tape recorder. Johnson conceptualized *John Somebody* in the context of rock music, and his use of an aggressive electric-guitar accompaniment grows from his wish to create a piece that is "as much about rock's iconography as its sounds," using the "emotional postures of popular songs" as "public models or templates against which listeners can match their private experiences." Popular singing has far more in common with the tones and textures of ordinary speech than operatic or *Lied* singing has, and *John Somebody* is (among other things) a commentary on the speechlike nature of rock vocalizing and on the aesthetic properties of the electronically modified instrumental sounds that have been coupled with rock singing throughout its history.

Johnson began composing *No Memory* by taking two seconds' worth of his own spontaneously recorded voice and altering the pitches of the recording with a harmonizer, in a process that yielded "a wide range of rhythmic/metric variations via the process of phasing." He then manipulated and "re-rationalized" this material, working it into rock-based rhythms that provided the basis for an electric-guitar score. Johnson sees this piece as "a picture of selective forgetting, of re-writing one's own history," as the original voice-elements mimic "unresolved, unprocessed memories of an event" by growing in various directions and moving "through a series of collisions and attempted resolutions." Along the way, the musically constructed voice-body appears to compel accompaniment from electric instruments that "must in the end settle for a direct orchestration of the opening voice-phrases; just as our most complex experiences, given time and re-telling, end up as just another story with a punch-line."

Although they employ different methods, Reich and Johnson both want to deconstruct traditional notions of composition by exploring a specifically *corporeal* dimension in the domain of through-composed music. Here again a productive set of dialectics and dialogics is in play. The division between "music" and "noise" has been radically questioned by John Cage and any number of musicians following in his wake, much as the division between "writing" and the arbitrary presence of printed words has been questioned by Burroughs and his ilk. Along related lines, an interest in musical "primitivism" cultivated by many modernists and postmodernists has encouraged a thoughtful concern for music as sound—often biologically rooted sound—as opposed to music as narrative, music as psychological expression, and other such conventional approaches.

A biological orientation in music does not necessarily entail the use of vocal sounds, as a few examples from Reich's work demonstrate. In two portions of *Music for Eighteen Musicians,* the phrasing of woodwind instruments is determined not by precise notation but by the instruction for each player to hold certain notes for the duration of "one gentle breath." Some sounds in *Drumming* are made by whistling and tongue clicking. *Clapping Music* is what its title says, with no extracorporeal instrumentation at all. And so forth.

Conversely, voices may be used in a manner that does not involve distorting their sounds, as Reich and Johnson do in the works discussed above, but subordinates sense (meaning) to sound (tone) by placing voices in the service of texts that are inherently disconnected from traditional notions of meaning and communication—i.e., by deploying the equivalent of Burroughs's disruptive cut-up and fold-in procedures at the time when the text is chosen or written rather than when it is recorded or sound-edited. A monumental instance of this is Philip Glass and Robert Wilson's use of a radically nonlinear (and often radically nonsensical) text in their masterpiece *Einstein on the Beach,* first performed in the mid-seventies and widely circulated since then in recorded versions.[53]

In addition to its musical score, this opera has both a sung "libretto" and a spoken "book."[54] The libretto consists of numbers (one, two, three . . .) and solfeggio syllables (do, re, mi . . .) that correspond with the rhythmic structures and melodic trajectories, respectively, of the score. The book is a series of spoken texts written by frequent Wilson collaborators, none of whom are "authors" in the usual sense. One is Lucinda Childs, a dancer and choreographer (often linked with the minimalist school) whose usual modes of artistic expression are gestic rather than verbal. Another is the late Samuel M. Johnson, a stage and recording performer who was chosen for the role of a judge in *Einstein* because of his physical appearance rather than his acting abilities. The most important is Christopher Knowles, a man medically diagnosed as autistic (or brain-damaged, by some reports) and valued as a partner by Wilson because of his ability to generate unconventional language structures (in writing, typing, and oral improvisation) based on spontaneous elisions, omissions, and additions that disrupt the expected flow of "normal" verbal activity.[55]

Texts by these "writers" are recited during the nonlinear, nonliterary action of *Einstein.* Occasionally they echo the onstage events, as when a motorist tells a story of lovers on a park bench while two figures on such a bench are visible; more often they take a parallel track that corresponds with the opera's visual events in terms of duration but not of literal meaning, as when Childs speaks a nonsensical monologue about an "air-conditioned supermarket" while lounging on a bisected bed in an abstractly designed courtroom. In all cases, it is clear that the purpose of the vocal performance is not to convey a set of literal meanings; rather, its function is to add purely textural elements (tone, timbre, grain of voice) to the complex sonic mixture constituted by the opera as a whole. Knowles's texts are the most interesting in this regard, since they call on the speaker to recite monologues with singularly "unimportant" content (e.g., the disc-jockey schedule of a New York radio station) in a theatrically sustained and thoroughly performative manner. In keeping with this agenda, Glass has slightly rearranged certain passages to make them consonant with the "additive" rhythmic structures that he frequently borrows from Indian music. For example:

> Would . . .
> Would I . . .
> Would I Get . . .
> Would I Get Some . . .
> Would I Get Some Wind . . .

and

> Bank robbery is punishable . . .
> Bank robbery is . . .

Bank robbery . . .
Bank robbery is punishable by . . .

Some others are so mechanically structured that simply reciting them in a musical context amounts to an exercise in minimalist vocalese. For example:

batch
catch
hatch
latch
match

Still others are written in such a destructured way that a "literal" recitation would be impossible if the performer did not make clear interpretive decisions as to how they should be spoken. For example:

Make a tiota on thses these are theiidays loop . . .

and

It could get the r ilroad for these workers. Itmmcould
So will it . . .

Wilson has used the term *weather* to describe the intended effect of such texts within his work—suggesting that their contributions are at once essential and peripheral, sonically inescapable and semiotically irrelevant, "too little" in the meanings they offer and perhaps "too much" in the demands they make on the attention spans of listeners accustomed to traditional music-theater texts. In recorded versions of the opera, these recitations work along with the voices of the performers who speak them—often (not always) the same individuals who wrote them—to construct invisible bodies whose mysteriousness thrives in direct proportion to the strangeness and arbitrariness of the near-aleatory texts being uttered.

Throughout the work, the spoken texts have been selected and contextualized in accord with Glass's predilection for abstract musical expression and Wilson's artistic impulse to employ words not as meaning-full signifiers but as free-floating objects—sonic *things* that convey pleasure by means of texture, volume, frequency, duration, and suchlike *physical* characteristics. In addition to registering vocally related traits of the persons who utter them, therefore, they construct depersonalized *implied* bodies that are at once wholly present in their textural sophistication and semiotic grotesquerie, and wholly absent insofar as they are residues of bygone creative moments when Wilson and Glass called for unmediated contributions from performers with little conventional sophistication in the aesthetics of the written text. Knowles's texts provide particularly forceful examples of ways in which Burroughs-like varieties of discontinuity and non sequitur can find intense expressive functions within a work devoted to making aesthetic unity from individual elements so diverse as to appear (if not actually to be) haphazardly selected and randomly combined. Like the other artists discussed here, Glass and Wilson have followed Burroughs's lead in subverting the myth of integrated consciousness by fashioning a vibrantly creative art object charged with celebratory recognition of the inherently decentered, disunified nature of the human subjects who perceive it.

Notes
Index

NOTES

Preface

1. For more on this important 1959 film and others mentioned here, see David Sterritt, *Mad to Be Saved: The Beats, the '50s, and Film* (Carbondale: Southern Illinois University Press, 1998).

1. Beats, Movies, and Ills of Postwar America

1. Dennis McNally, *Desolate Angel: Jack Kerouac, the Beat Generation, and America* (New York: Delta, 1990), 109.

2. Judith Clavir Albert and Stewart Edward Albert, *The Sixties Papers: Documents of a Rebellious Decade* (New York: Praeger, 1984), 7.

3. When asked by the National Opinion Research Center whether they "think most Negroes in the United States are being treated fairly or unfairly," a majority of people (63 percent) answered "fairly" in both 1946 and 1956. Hazel Gaudet Erskine, "The Polls: Race Relations," *Public Opinion Quarterly* 26 (1962): 139; cited by Thomas F. Pettigrew, "Parallel and Distinctive Changes in Anti-Semitic and Anti-Negro Attitudes," in *Jews in the Mind of America,* by Charles Herbert Stember and others (New York: Basic Books, 1966), 380. Pettigrew notes that the consistency of this 1946–56 response pattern does not conflict with a separate finding of reduction in antiblack prejudice during the same period, since the question about fair treatment "does not correlate well with known measures of prejudice" (399n). This clearly indicates the ability of subjects to engage in acts of mental compartmentalization that have the effect of separating awareness of their own personal biases from their perceptions of social equity in the culture of which they are a part.

4. Todd Gitlin, *The Sixties: Years of Hope, Days of Rage* (Toronto: Bantam Books, 1987), 61.

5. Harold E. Quinley and Charles Y. Glock, *Anti-Semitism in America* (New York: The Free Press, 1979), 19.

6. Charles Herbert Stember in Stember and others, *Jews in the Mind of America,* 64–65, and Morton Keller, "Jews and the Character of American Life since 1930," in the same volume (268, 271). Stember finds the decline in positive and negative generalizations about Jews to be "a clear gain," since it indicates that Jews are being viewed "less stereotypically" than before. Keller, linking the relative absence of anti-Semitism with the Communist scare of the early fifties and the civil-rights movement of the sixties, sees it as evidence that Jews occupied a "subordinate place in the American consciousness" during the period; later he suggests that "a new and difficult condition which might be called *asemitism* . . . indifference to, or unawareness of, their identity as Jews" is a problem to which Jews should turn their attention in order to preserve "their individuality from the oppressive weight of cultural sameness" (emphasis in original).

7. Henry Popkin, "The Vanishing Jew of Our Popular Culture," *Commentary* (July 1952): 46–55; cited in Judith E. Doneson, *The Holocaust in American Film* (Philadelphia: Jewish Publication Society, 1987), 65.

8. Doneson, *Holocaust in American Film,* 82–83.

9. Quinley and Glock, *Anti-Semitism in America,* xi.

10. Pettigrew, "Parallel and Distinctive Changes," 398.

11. Bruno Bettelheim and Morris Janowitz, *Social Change and Prejudice, Including Dynamics of Prejudice* (New York: The Free Press, 1964), 147.

12. Ibid., 262–63. Bettelheim and Janowitz see these phenomena as reasons "why external controls, as the creations, representations, or symbols of superego demands, lend support to the discrimination of [i.e., discrimination against] those groups on whom id tendencies are displaced, while they mitigate the discrimination of groups on whom reaction-formations against id tendencies are displaced."

13. Pettigrew, "Parallel and Distinctive Changes," 385–86.

14. Donald Bogle, *Toms, Coons, Mulattoes, Mammies, and Bucks: An Interpretive History of Blacks in American Films* (New York: Continuum, 1991), 159–93.

15. Like many of his analyses of specific films, Bogle's photo captions tend to weaken his attempts to paint the fifties as a progressive decade for African Americans in Hollywood cinema. He writes, for example, "Even in the 1950s, black shoulders were made to cry on," under a picture of black Ethel Waters embracing and comforting white Julie Harris in *The Member of the Wedding* (1952).

16. Thus, in effect, the film industry "blacklisted Jews in front of the camera as well as behind it." Lester Friedman, *Hollywood's Image of the Jew* (New York: Frederick Ungar, 1982), 135, 142.

17. Patricia Erens, *The Jew in American Cinema* (Bloomington: Indiana University Press, 1984), 200, 204, 228.

18. Ilan Avisar, *Screening the Holocaust: Cinema's Images of the Unspeakable* (Bloomington: Indiana University Press, 1988), 130–33.

19. Doneson, *Holocaust in American Film,* 82–83, 61.

20. Annette Insdorf, *Indelible Shadows: Film and the Holocaust* (New York: Vintage Books, 1983), 7, 10.

21. E. E. Cohen, "The Film as a Social Force," *Commentary* 4, no. 2 (October 1947), 113; quoted in Avisar, *Screening the Holocaust,* 107. Avisar also finds subtextual resonance in a scene in *Crossfire* showing the police officer persuading a young soldier to cooperate with the law. A statement by the policeman on anti-Semitism and racism only elicits the soldier's suspicion that his questioner may be a Jew himself, so the policeman tells him the poignant story of an old man who was murdered solely because of his Irish-Catholic background—thus reflecting an apparent conviction among the film's makers that American audiences would find it more plausible for the soldier to sympathize with an Irish person than with a Jew (106–7).

22. Describing both *Gentleman's Agreement* and *Crossfire* as "extremely naive and even phony in their overall optimistic structure," Avisar adds that "their message is spurious and even dubious" with regard to the anti-Semitic bigotry that is their ostensible theme. The former film "suggests that it is wrong to hate Jews, but at the same time it presents them as different people, and the presentation actually conforms to many derogatory stereotypical views. The lesson of Kazan and Peck's movie was best summarized by one spectator who declared, 'Henceforth I'm always going to be good to Jewish people because you can never tell when they will turn out to be Gentiles.' But when they were released, *Crossfire* and *Gentleman's Agreement* were considered artistically successful and were received with positive and encouraging public reaction." Avisar, *Screening the Holocaust,* 109.

23. Avisar identifies Henry Hathaway's *The Desert Fox* (1951) as the first movie that "portrayed a Nazi in an unambiguous, positive way," referring to its depiction of Field Marshall Erwin Rommell, the German military commander. Citing a *Films in Review* critic who stated in 1951 that "all students of World War II . . . will be pleased by the [film's] amount of documented history," Avisar posits the likely identity of such "students" as members of "the revisionist school, whose arguments range from a denial of the existence of death camps to a complete exoneration of the perpetrators of the Nazi atrocities." Avisar goes on to point out Dmytryk's *The Young Lions* (1958), about a German officer and two young American soldiers, as a crystallization of the "salient characteristics of the war movies of the fifties—diffusing the antagonism between former enemies, American self-flagellation, blind condemnation of war and its anonymous

engineers, and sympathy with defeated enemies," all of which lead to a "disregard for moral realities of history" that render the film (and its ilk) profoundly objectionable from any standpoint that is effectively cognizant of past and present Jewish difficulties in the American sociocultural sphere (110–11, 116). The review referred to is by Henry Hart, *Films in Review* 2, no. 8 (October 1951): 50–51 (ellipsis in Avisar's quotation). Erens also finds that "redemption" and "whitewashing" of Nazis became fashionable in Hollywood films during the fifties (*Jew in American Cinema,* 223).

24. Ted Morgan, *Literary Outlaw: The Life and Times of William S. Burroughs* (New York: Avon Books, 1990), 288.

25. McNally, *Desolate Angel,* 109.

26. Michael Schumacher, *Dharma Lion: A Critical Biography of Allen Ginsberg* (New York: St. Martin's Press, 1992), 363. For discussion of dialogic and monologic literature, see M. M. Bakhtin, *The Dialogic Imagination: Four Essays,* trans. Caryl Emerson and Michael Holquist (Austin: University of Texas Press, 1981), and *Problems of Dostoevsky's Poetics,* trans. Caryl Emerson (Minneapolis: University of Minnesota Press, 1984).

27. Gerald Nicosia, *Memory Babe: A Critical Biography of Jack Kerouac* (London: Penguin Books, 1983), 415. Ironically, the *Li'l Abner* comic strip was created by Al Capp, an outspoken figure of the midcentury far right.

28. Jack Kerouac, *Vanity of Duluoz: An Adventurous Education, 1935–46* (1968; reprint, New York: Penguin Books, 1994), 38.

29. Barry Miles, *Ginsberg: A Biography* (New York: Simon and Schuster, 1989), 422. Ginsberg must have rationalized away a great deal of awful stuff. He once recalled Kerouac criticizing him for being involved with political activists Abby Hoffman and Jerry Rubin, for instance, saying, "Ginsberg, what are you hanging around with all those dirty Jew Communists for, anyway?" A few years earlier, in 1964, he wrote in a journal entry, "I had cut [Kerouac] off the phone yesterday dawn when he began repeating some accusations against Jews—'All the bureaucrats of Soviet Hungary are Jewish'—called drunk, I was sleepy." (421, 336). Also visible here is Kerouac's weird streak of anticommunist conservatism.

30. McNally, *Desolate Angel,* 293. McNally adds that a few days later, Ginsberg tried to counter Kerouac's anti-Semitism by the peculiar tactic of listing his Jewish friends, weighing sympathetic Jews like Lucien Carr and Gilbert Millstein against others like Norman Podhoretz and Robert Brustein; the latter group included Albert Zugsmith, who had produced the Hollywood exploitation movie *The Beat Generation* a couple of years earlier, incidentally co-opting that title and making it unavailable for the avant-garde film *Pull My Daisy,* directed by Robert Frank and Alfred

Lesley in 1958, with which Kerouac himself was involved. Kerouac did not benefit from Ginsberg's exercise, being "too soggily emotional to be reasonable" at the time (294).

31. Quoted in Nicosia, *Memory Babe,* 555.

32. Quoted in Morgan, *Literary Outlaw,* 554–55. Morgan also cites a 1940 incident when Burroughs muttered, "Hitler was perfectly right," after a wealthy Jewish woman steered him to the servants' entrance when he was working as a delivery person; the biographer explains this in class terms, arguing that since Burroughs had such a "fragile" sense of his own status, "any episode that linked him with the underclass was sure to make him seethe" (77).

33. Quoted in Schumacher, *Dharma Lion,* 403.

34. Barry Miles, *William Burroughs: El Hombre Invisible—A Portrait* (New York: Hyperion, 1993), 102–3.

35. Jack Kerouac, *On the Road* (1957; reprint, New York: Penguin Books, 1991), 180.

36. Jack Kerouac, *The Subterraneans* (1958; reprint, New York: Grove Weidenfeld, 1989), 16.

37. Kerouac, *Subterraneans,* 7; emphasis in original.

38. Nicosia has described this "life" as "mostly a fantasy of himself [Kerouac] living like [novelist William] Faulkner on a homestead in the Deep South, discussing literature with some genteel doctor over a bottle of Old Granddad." *Memory Babe,* 445.

39. Kerouac, *Subterraneans,* 17.

40. *The Subterraneans* was produced for MGM by Arthur Freed and directed by Ranald MacDougall from Robert Thom's screenplay. George Peppard played the protagonist, with Janice Rule, Roddy McDowall, Scott Marlowe, Jim Hutton, and Arte Johnson also in the cast. "This is their story told to the hot rhythms of fabulous jazz!" boasts a one-sheet poster for the movie, and the film indeed shows a taste in jazz more Beat-like than that of many Beat-related movies; its excellent musicians include Gerry Mulligan, Shelly Manne, Art Farmer, Art Pepper, Red Mitchell, Carmen McRae, and André Previn. Song titles include "Coffee Time," "Look Ma, No Clothes," and "Analyst."

2. Lisped, Muxed, and Completely Flunk: Jack Kerouac Meets the Three Stooges

1. Stan Brakhage, *Film at Wit's End: Eight Avant-Garde Filmmakers* (Kingston, N.Y.: McPherson, 1989), 143.

2. For a more expansive discussion of points made in the first portion of this essay, see David Sterritt, *Mad to Be Saved: The Beats, the '50s, and Film* (Carbondale: Southern Illinois University Press, 1998).

3. Mikhail Bakhtin, *Problems of Dostoevsky's Poetics,* trans. Caryl

Emerson (Minneapolis: University of Minnesota Press, 1984), 122–26. Emphases in original.

4. Ibid., 129–30. Emphasis in original.

5. Mikhail Bakhtin, *Rabelais and His World,* trans. Hélène Iswolsky (Bloomington: Indiana University Press, 1984), 118.

6. Regina Weinreich, *The Spontaneous Poetics of Jack Kerouac: A Study of the Fiction* (New York: Paragon House, 1990), 120, 122.

7. Bakhtin, *Problems of Dostoevsky's Poetics,* 124, 126, 127; emphasis in original.

8. Ibid., 126.

9. Jack Kerouac, *Doctor Sax: Faust Part Three* (1959; reprinted, New York: Grove Weidenfeld, 1987), 4. Weinreich also cites this passage as exemplary of Kerouac's method.

10. M. M. Bakhtin, "Forms of Time and of the Chronotope in the Novel: Notes Toward a Historical Poetics," in *The Dialogic Imagination: Four Essays,* trans. Caryl Emerson and Michael Holquist (Austin: University of Texas Press, 1981), 193.

11. Ibid., 177.

12. Ibid., 170.

13. Jack Kerouac, *Vanity of Duluoz: An Adventurous Education, 1935–46* (New York: Coward-McCann, 1968).

14. This is where Kerouac had been called to identify David Kammerer's body after Lucien Carr killed him during a sexual struggle in 1944, one of the most tragic incidents connected with the early Beat scene.

15. Kerouac, *Vanity of Duluoz,* 279–80.

16. Gregory Stephenson, *The Daybreak Boys: Essays on the Literature of the Beat Generation* (Carbondale: Southern Illinois University Press, 1990), 48.

17. John Tytell, *Naked Angels: The Lives & Literature of the Beat Generation* (New York: McGraw-Hill Book Company, 1976), 141.

18. Jack Kerouac, "Essentials of Spontaneous Prose," *Evergreen Review* 2, no. 5 (1968). Copyrighted by Kerouac in 1958. Reprinted in Ann Charters, *The Portable Beat Reader* (New York: Viking, 1992), 57–58. It is striking how neatly this brief catalogue of writing tips recapitulates Sigmund Freud's three-part schema of the stages of human sexual development.

19. Bakhtin, *Rabelais and His World,* 24, 25, 26.

20. Kerouac, *Vanity of Duluoz,* 273.

21. Gerald Nicosia, *Memory Babe: A Critical Biography of Jack Kerouac* (London: Penguin Books, 1983), 405.

22. Kerouac, *Doctor Sax,* 18–19.

23. Ibid., 67, 82, 149 (second ellipsis in original), 162.

24. Ibid., 204.

25. Bakhtin, *Rabelais and His World,* 368–69.

26. Jack Kerouac, *Visions of Cody* (1972; reprinted, New York: Penguin, 1993), 76–77.

27. Ibid., 10–11.

28. Allen Ginsberg, "The Great Rememberer," introduction to *Visions of Cody,* by Jack Kerouac (New York: McGraw-Hill, 1972), vii.

29. Weinreich, *Spontaneous Poetics of Jack Kerouac,* 70–71, 68.

30. Kerouac, *Visions of Cody,* 11.

31. Ibid., 76–77.

32. Ibid., 281.

33. Ibid., 279. The heroine of this episode, here given a momentary change of name, is also known as Joan Clawthighs at one point.

34. Ibid., 276.

35. Ibid., 282.

36. Ibid., 290.

37. Ibid., 304.

38. Ibid., 305.

39. Ibid., 304; emphasis in original. Kerouac is, of course, riffing on a popular old song here.

40. Douglas Kahn, "Death in Light of the Phonograph: Raymond Roussel's *Locus Solus,*" in *Wireless Imagination: Sound, Radio, and the Avant-Garde,* ed. Douglas Kahn and Gregory Whitehead (Cambridge: MIT Press, 1992), 69–103, cited at 93–94. Jacques Derrida notes a related operation in his deconstruction of Jean-Jacques Rousseau: "Within the voice, the presence of the object already disappears. The self-presence of the voice and of the [hearing-oneself-speak] conceals the very thing that visible space allows to be placed before us. The thing disappearing, the voice substitutes an acoustic sign for it which can, in the place of the object taken away, penetrate profoundly into me. . . . It is the only way of interiorizing the phenomenon . . . but which . . . supposes that the disappearance of presence in the form of the object, the being-before-the-eyes or being-at-hand, installs a sort of fiction, if not a lie, at the very origin of speech." Jacques Derrida, *Of Grammatology,* trans. Gayatri Chakravorty Spivak (Baltimore: Johns Hopkins University Press, 1976), 240.

41. Kahn, "Death in Light of the Phonograph," 93, 103.

42. Antonin Artaud, *To Have Done with the Judgment of God,* trans. Clayton Eshleman, reprinted in Kahn and Whitehead, *Wireless Imagination,* 309–29, cited at 309.

43. Jack Kerouac, *Big Sur* (New York: Penguin Books, 1981), 231–32. Also of interest here is Kerouac's poem "Old Angel Midnight," long unpublished in its complete form. Kerouac biographer Dennis McNally calls it an attempt "to catch the sound of all tongues, the infinite sound of the universe as it floated into his window late at night." Written in an uncharacteristically chaotic scribble, it is "devoid of meaning in the common sense, a high argument between Jack and God in a universe of hur-

ricane winds that swept his words around like confetti. St. Benedict conversed with Danny and the Juniors, while Carolyn and Burroughs made love in the midst of Buddhist lore." Dennis McNally, *Desolate Angel: Jack Kerouac, the Beat Generation, and America* (New York: Delta, 1990), 216–17. The poem was called "Lucien Midnight" until Lucien Carr objected.

44. Of particular note is the frequency of /k/ sounds in such utterances by Artaud and Kerouac alike. See the excerpt from "Sea" cited here or this example of Artaud's glossolalia in a letter written from the asylum at Rodez where he was confined for many years:

> ortura ortura konara
> kokona kokona koma
> kurbura kurbura kurbura
> kurbata kurbata keyna
> pesti anti pestantum putara
> pest anti pestantum putra

(Letter to Henri Parisot, 1945, published in *Antonin Artaud: Selected Writings,* ed. Susan Sontag and trans. Helen Weaver [Berkeley: University of California Press, 1988], 451.) Looking at Artaud's late work through Roland Barthes's idea of the "grain of the voice" and Artaud's own fascination with conflating the mouth and the anus, theorist Allen S. Weiss calls attention to Artaud's ingenuity in forging a linkage between these anatomical parts that is "not merely symbolic" but deploys glottal sounds as a "symbolic—and physiognomic—reflection of defecation," since closure of the glottis in speech constitutes a material echo of sphincter activity in anal functioning. Weiss adds, "The glottic sphincter permits the physical and symbolic articulation of oral and anal rejection (and retention)" through vocalizations that are "screams of the entire body and not just the mouth." (Allen S. Weiss, "Radio, Death, and the Devil: Artaud's *Pour en finir avec le jugement de dieu,*" in Kahn and Whitehead, *Wireless Imagination,* 288–89.) It is interesting to consider these matters in light of Bakhtin's praise of Rabelais for recuperating the material bodily lower stratum and devising a novelistic language that allows for material rather than merely symbolic contact between author and reader; and to compare Artaud's efforts toward a language-body linkage with Kerouac's association of writing with scatological and seminal production, as in his "Essentials of Spontaneous Prose," quoted earlier.

45. Artaud, *To Have Done with the Judgment of God,* 316.

46. Antonin Artaud, "Insanity and Black Magic," from *Artaud le Mômo,* reprinted in Sontag, *Antonin Artaud,* 529–31, cited at 530.

47. Artaud, *To Have Done with the Judgment of God,* 328–29.

48. This association is not surprising since for Artaud the soma, in Mikhail Yampolsky's words, "begins where differentiation and articulation end. . . . The nondifferentiation of the body's integument, its lack of

divisions or boundaries, corresponds to the indissolubility of sound." Mikhail Yampolsky, "Voice Devoured: Artaud and Borges on Dubbing," *October* 64 (spring 1993): 57–77, cited at 59.

49. Antonin Artaud, "The Premature Old Age of the Cinema," in Sontag, *Antonin Artaud,* 311–14, cited at 314.

50. Antonin Artaud, "On *The Seashell and the Clergyman,*" in Sontag, *Antonin Artaud,* 149–52, cited at 151–52.

51. Artaud, "Premature Old Age of the Cinema," 314.

52. "Wherever the *machine* is/there is always the abyss and the void,/ there is a technical intervention that distorts and annihilates what one has done./. . ./this is why I am through with Radio. . . ." (Antonin Artaud, Letter to Paule Thévenin, 1948, in Sontag, *Antonin Artaud,* 584; emphasis in original.) Susan Sontag asserts that while Artaud "never entirely stopped hoping to use activities in the arts as a means of spiritual liberation, art was always suspect—like the body." Hence, it was not medium-specific properties of film or radio but the inherent mediations of art itself (at least, as conceived by humanity so far) that were the trouble. (See Sontag, "Artaud," in Sontag, *Antonin Artaud,* l.) Kerouac displayed some hostility of his own toward radio, incidentally. In the "118th Chorus" of *Mexico City Blues,* he speaks of "The radio I dont wanta hear/And cant have to hear," and the "119th Chorus" begins,

> Self be your lantern,
> Self be your guide—
> Thus Spake Tathagata
> Warning of radios
> That would come
> Some day
> And make people
> Listen to automatic
> Words of others
> and the general flash of noises,
> forgetting self, not-self—
> Forgetting the secret. . . .

(Jack Kerouac, *Mexico City Blues* [1959; reprinted, New York: Grove Weidenfeld, 1990], 119; final ellipsis in original.)

53. Gregory Whitehead, "Out of the Dark: Notes on the Nobodies of Radio Art," in Kahn and Whitehead, *Wireless Imagination,* 253–63, cited at 261; line divisions restored. Herman Melville, a great favorite of the Beats, writes in *Moby-Dick:* "The lightning flashes through my skull; mine eye-balls ache and ache; my whole beaten brain seems as beheaded, and rolling on some stunning ground." The verse by Artaud is from *Artaud le Mômo.*

54. On states of liminality and ambiguous identity, see Richard

Schechner, *Between Theater & Anthropology* (Philadelphia: University of Pennsylvania Press, 1985), esp. chapter 2, "Restoration of Behavior."

55. Gilles Deleuze and Félix Guattari, *Anti-Oedipus: Capitalism and Schizophrenia,* trans. Robert Hurley, Mark Seem, and Helen R. Lane (Minneapolis: University of Minnesota Press, 1983), 132–33.

56. Ibid., 277–78.

3. *Desolation Angels:* Kerouac, Buddhism, and Film

1. It has also been suggested that Kerouac discovered Buddhism later, in the library of his Lowell, Massachusetts, hometown in late 1952 or early 1953, since he doesn't delve into Buddhist ideas in his early writing.

2. Jack Kerouac, *Desolation Angels* (1965; reprinted, New York: Perigee Books, 1980). The passages cited below are from pp. 69–70, 72, and 77, respectively.

3. Allen Ginsberg, "Negative Capability: Kerouac's Buddhist Ethic." *Tricycle: The Buddhist Review* 2, no. 1 (1992): 8–13, cited at 8. Adapted by Ginsberg (for a column in this journal called "Ancestors") from an essay in Pierre Anctil, ed., *Un Homme Grand: Jack Kerouac à la Confluence des Cultures* (Ottawa: Carleton University Press, 1990).

4. Roger J. Corless, "Buddhism and the West," in *Buddhism: A Modern Perspective,* ed. Charles S. Prebish (University Park: Pennsylvania State University Press, 1975), 251. Corless states that Spengler's work *Der Untergang des Abendlandes* is recounted "in a Buddhist manner."

5. Kerouac's long involvement with Buddhism, however, never succeeded in expunging Christianity from his belief system. In the highly Buddhistic novel *Desolation Angels,* he refers to Buddha as "(my hero) (my *other* hero, Christ is first)" (259), and in the "Negative Capability" essay, Ginsberg confirms on a biographical level that as Kerouac grew older, "in despair and lacking the means to calm his mind and let go of the suffering, he tended more and more to grasp at the Cross . . . finally conceiving of himself as being crucified" (13). Not everyone would agree with Ginsberg's assessment of Kerouac's depth as a Buddhist devotee, moreover. Warren French cites the observation of Buddhist thinker and Beat associate Philip Whalen that Kerouac's interest in Buddhism was always "pretty much literary" and uses Kerouac's negative reaction to three months of wilderness solitude in 1956 as evidence of his "lack of a disposition toward the contemplative life." Warren French, *Jack Kerouac* (Boston: Twayne Publishers, 1986), 15. (The observation by Whalen comes from Barry Gifford and Lawrence Lee, *Jack's Book: An Oral Biography of Jack Kerouac.*)

6. Ginsberg, "Negative Capability," 10, 9.

7. Lewis R. Lancaster, "The Prajnaparamita Literature," in Prebish, *Buddhism,* 71.

8. Ginsberg, "Negative Capability," 12.

9. Quoted in ibid., 13. From Jack Kerouac, "The Last Word," *Escapade* 3 (spring 1959).

10. Douglas M. Burns, "Nirvana, Nihilism and Satori," in *Pathways of Buddhist Thought,* ed. Nyanaponika Mahathera (New York: Barnes & Noble, 1972), 172–73.

11. Daisetz Teitaro Suzuki, *The Awakening of Zen* (Boulder: Prajna Press, 1980), 36.

12. So crucial is this practice to the semiotic construction of classical cinema that Gilles Deleuze suggests "it is montage itself which constitutes the whole, and thus gives us the image *of* time. It is therefore the principle act of cinema. Time . . . flows from the montage which links one movement-image to another." He goes on to cite the insistence of Soviet filmmaker and theorist Sergei Eisenstein that "montage must proceed by alterations, conflicts, resolutions, and resonances, in short an activity of selection and co-ordination, in order to give time its real dimension, and the whole its consistency"; and he follows this with the observation of Italian filmmaker and theorist Pier Paolo Pasolini that "montage has the property of . . . achieving time" by virtue of its selection and coordination of "significant moments." Gilles Deleuze, *Cinema 2: The Time-Image,* trans. Hugh Tomlinson and Robert Galeta (Minneapolis: University of Minnesota Press, 1989), 34–35, 36; emphasis in original. Pasolini is quoted from his *L'Expérience Héretique* (Lausanne: Payot, 1976).

13. Eisenstein states that "it is precisely the *montage* principle . . . which obliges spectators themselves to *create* and the montage principle, by this means, achieves that great power of inner creative excitement in the *spectator.* . . ." Sergei M. Eisenstein, *The Film Sense,* trans. Jay Leyda (San Diego: Harcourt Brace Jovanovich, 1942), 35; emphasis in original. See also Eisenstein's description of the artistic experience whereby an image "is born and grown" within the spectator. "Not only the author has created, but I also—the creating spectator—have participated," he writes (34). Also relevant is Jacques Aumont's observation that each of Eisenstein's own films contains "a *system* of fragments" and that "it could almost be said that the fragment does not exist outside of this system of its relations to the other fragments (to the whole of the text). The idea that it could be autonomized and extracted as a unit of meaning is completely contrary to that constant preoccupation with the systematic. . . ." Jacques Aumont, *Montage Eisenstein,* trans. Lee Hildreth, Constance Penley, and Andrew Ross (Bloomington: Indiana University Press, 1985), 35–36; emphasis in original.

14. The modalities in question often appear to be dualistic when first encountered, but Zen Buddhism seeks to transcend binary conceptualization through the notion of *sunyata* or emptiness. "All opposites rise from it, sink into it, exist in it," writes one authority. Suzuki, *Awakening of Zen,* 81.

15. Jack Kerouac, *Book of Dreams* (San Francisco: City Lights Books, 1961), 4.

16. Even such a theorist as Christian Metz, who insists on a fundamental discontinuity between dreaming and cinema viewing, has observed that such physical conditions as reduced motor activity and an environment free of ambient sound, joined with such psychological conditions as film's encouragement of narcissistic withdrawal and "indulgence of phantasy," may heighten the film spectator's "affective participation" and "perceptual transference" to such a degree that "consciousness of the filmic situation as such starts to become a bit murky and to waver," resulting in a somewhat dreamlike experience for the moviegoer. Christian Metz, *The Imaginary Signifier: Psychoanalysis and the Cinema,* trans. Celia Britton and others (Bloomington: Indiana University Press, 1982), 101–7.

17. Jacques Derrida, *Writing and Difference,* trans. Alan Bass (Chicago: University of Chicago Press, 1978), 48, 51; emphases in original. Derrida is analyzing the discussion of René Descartes by Michel Foucault in *Madness and Civilization: A History of Insanity in the Age of Reason.* Derrida attributes the phrase "objective value" to M. Gueroult.

18. Regina Weinreich, *The Spontaneous Poetics of Jack Kerouac: A Study of the Fiction* (New York: Paragon House, 1990), 75–76, 80–81. See also Jack Kerouac, *Visions of Cody* (1972; reprinted, New York: Penguin Books, 1993).

19. From the *Prajnaparamita,* or "Highest Perfect Wisdom," portion of the *Heart Sutra* as adapted by Ginsberg and Gelek Rinpoche from Shunryu Suzuki Roshi's translation. Ginsberg, "Negative Capability," 11.

20. Gerald Nicosia, *Memory Babe: A Critical Biography of Jack Kerouac* (London: Penguin Books, 1983), 402.

21. Jack Kerouac, "183rd Chorus," in *Mexico City Blues* (1959; reprinted, New York: Grove Weidenfeld, 1990), 183.

4. Revision, Prevision, and the Aura of Improvisatory Art

1. John Clellon Holmes, "The Great Rememberer," in *Nothing More to Declare* (New York: Dutton, 1967); quoted in Scott Donaldson, ed., *Jack Kerouac: On the Road—Text and Criticism* (Harmondsworth: Penguin Books, 1979), 590.

2. Jack Kerouac, "The Last Word," *Escapade,* December 1960, 104; quoted in Tom Clark, *Jack Kerouac: A Biography* (New York: Paragon House, 1990), 102.

3. Jack Kerouac, "Belief & Technique for Modern Prose," *Evergreen Review* 2, no. 8 (spring 1959): 57.

4. Nat Shapiro and Nat Hentoff, *Hear Me Talkin' to Ya* (New York: Dover, 1966), 147, 157–58; quoted in James Lincoln Collier, *Jazz: The American Theme Song* (New York: Oxford University Press, 1993), 49,

43. The quotations from jazz musicians that I cite in this essay, extracted from readily available books on the subject, are meant to be representative and illustrative rather than particularly articulate or astute.

5. Barry Kernfeld, "Improvisation," in *The New Grove Dictionary of Jazz,* ed. Barry Kernfeld (New York: St. Martin's Press, 1994), 561.

6. Ibid., 554.

7. Allen Ginsberg, "A Conversation," in *Composed on the Tongue: Literary Conversations, 1967–1977* (San Francisco: Grey Fox Press, 1980), 94.

8. Holmes, "Great Rememberer," 589.

9. Kernfeld, "Improvisation," 554.

10. *American Heritage Dictionary,* 4th ed.

11. Walter Benjamin, "The Work of Art in the Age of Mechanical Reproduction," in *Illuminations,* trans. Harry Zohn (New York: Schocken Books, 1985), 221, 223, 243n. 5.

12. Although recordings on wax cylinders were produced as early as 1877, critic Morley Jones notes that recorded music did not become widely available "until the emergence of Victor and Columbia as major record labels in 1902," the same year in which pianist Jelly Roll Morton later claimed (dubiously but colorfully) to have "invented" jazz. See Alan Rich, ed., *Jazz* (New York: Simon and Schuster, 1980), 2–3.

13. As always when artistic practice is being discussed, generalities and labels should not be taken too literally; while big-band jazz and bebop differed in important ways, there was in fact a species of big-band bebop, exemplified by 1940s bands of Dizzy Gillespie and Woody Herman, among others. See Thomas Owens, *Bebop: The Music and Its Players* (New York: Oxford University Press, 1994), 20–21.

14. Quotations from *Columbia Disc Digest,* July 1948, 3, 5; reprinted in "Celebrating the Fiftieth Anniversary of the LP," album booklet, Sony Classical–Masterworks Heritage CD (MHK 63327), 29, 32. The long-playing record was born during the same postwar years that witnessed the rise of bebop.

15. This method is related to other musical combinations of the *precomposed* and the *extemporaneous*—e.g., the keyboard continuo of the baroque period—that can be traced back to much earlier times.

16. As a bonus, the radical reworking of commonplace show-business material allowed African American bop players—of whom there were many, even though the style's audience was largely white—to carnivalize, ironize, and personalize products of mainstream culture, a particular pleasure after their years of oscillating between assimilationism and marginalization during the big-band era.

17. Daniel Belgrad, *The Culture of Spontaneity: Improvisation and the Arts in Postwar America* (Chicago: University of Chicago Press, 1998), 180.

18. Collier, *Jazz,* 51, 54–55. An exception to the principle of a basic jazz "vocabulary" is found in "free" or "outside" jazz, which extends melodies "outside" even the implied pitches of the harmonic series or ignores the concept of chord progressions altogether.

19. Owens, *Bebop,* 30.

20. Kernfeld, "Improvisation," 558; see 555–61 for various types of improvisational techniques and procedures.

21. Quoted in Dennis McNally, *Desolate Angel: Jack Kerouac, The Beat Generation, and America* (New York: Delta, 1990), 82.

22. Jack Kerouac, "Essentials of Spontaneous Prose," *Evergreen Review* 2, no. 5 (1968). Copyrighted by Kerouac in 1958. Reprinted in Ann Charters, *The Portable Beat Reader* (New York: Viking, 1992), 57–58, cited at 58.

23. James T. Jones, *A Map of* Mexico City Blues: *Jack Kerouac as Poet* (Carbondale: Southern Illinois University Press, 1992), 146–47.

24. Quoted in Arthur Knight and Kit Knight, eds., *The Beat Journey,* The Unspeakable Visions of the Individual, vol. 8 (California, Pa.: A. and K. Knight, 1978); cited in Clark, *Jack Kerouac,* 102.

25. William Burroughs, "The Cut-Up Method of Brion Gysin," *Re/Search* 4, no. 5 (1982): 36.

26. Quoted in Barry Miles, *Ginsberg: A Biography* (New York: Simon and Schuster, 1989), 188.

27. Burroughs, "Cut-Up Method of Brion Gysin," 35.

28. William S. Burroughs, "Journey Through Time-Space," in *The Job: Interviews with William S. Burroughs,* by Daniel Odier (New York: Penguin Books, 1989), 48, 56.

29. Henry Miller, preface to *The Subterraneans,* by Jack Kerouac (1958; reprint, New York: Grove Weidenfeld, 1989); quoted in John Tytell, *Naked Angels: The Lives & Literature of the Beat Generation* (New York: McGraw-Hill, 1976), 200.

30. Kerouac, "Belief & Technique for Modern Prose," 57.

31. Kerouac, "Essentials of Spontaneous Prose," 57; emphasis in original.

32. Ibid.

33. Regina Weinreich, *The Spontaneous Poetics of Jack Kerouac: A Study of the Fiction* (New York: Paragon House, 1990), 120, 5.

34. Jones, *Map of* Mexico City Blues, 151; see also Gerald Nicosia, *Memory Babe: A Critical Biography of Jack Kerouac* (New York: Penguin Books, 1983), 521 (emphasis in original). The title of Nicosia's book, referring to Kerouac's childhood nickname, is revealing in this context. He also notes (and Jones also cites) the fact that Kerouac's memorization of "extensive passages" from plays by William Shakespeare had been allowed to "filter into his spontaneous prose," suggesting that Kerouac's

literary memories were another imported element in his allegedly individualistic prose (500).

35. Jack Kerouac, "On the Road Again," *New Yorker* (June 22 and 29, 1998): 56; Jack Kerouac, *On the Road* (1957; reprint, New York: Penguin Books, 1991), 180–81.

36. Some avant-garde filmmakers have brought improvisation into the area of exhibition as well as production. An example is Ken Jacobs, who specifies that an AM radio (tuned to speech rather than music) be played during every screening of his 1959–63 film *Blonde Cobra;* while he gives very specific instructions about when (and how loud) the radio should be played, he obviously has no control over what audiences will hear on any given occasion.

37. Interview with Jean-Luc Godard, *Cahiers du Cinéma* 138 (December 1962). Reprinted in Jean Narboni and Tom Milne, eds., *Godard on Godard* (New York: Da Capo Press, 1986), 172–73.

38. Ibid., 180, 186.

39. Ibid., 186, 174.

40. Quoted in Penelope Gilliatt, "The Urgent Whisper," *New Yorker* (25 October 1976). Reprinted in *Jean-Luc Godard: Interviews,* ed. David Sterritt (Jackson: University Press of Mississippi, 1998), 78–79.

41. Quoted in Gene Youngblood, "Jean-Luc Godard: No Difference Between Life and Cinema," *Los Angeles Free Press* 15 March 1968. Reprinted in Sterritt, *Jean-Luc Godard,* 24.

42. Ibid., 29.

43. Quoted in Jonathan Cott, "Godard: Born-Again Filmmaker," *Rolling Stone* (27 November 1980). Reprinted in Sterritt, *Jean-Luc Godard,* 92.

44. Quoted in Gideon Bachmann, "The Carrots Are Cooked: A Conversation with Jean-Luc Godard," *Film Quarterly* 27, no. 3 (1984). Reprinted in Sterritt, *Jean-Luc Godard,* 129–30.

45. Jean-Luc Godard, "Montage My Fine Care." *Cahiers du Cinéma* 65 (December 1956). Reprinted in Narboni and Milne, *Godard on Godard,* 40.

46. This idea is strongly associated with critic and theorist André Bazin, one of Godard's early mentors.

47. Interview with Godard, *Cahiers du Cinéma.* Reprinted in Narboni and Milne, *Godard on Godard,* 173.

48. Quoted in Youngblood, "Jean-Luc Godard." Reprinted in Sterritt, *Jean-Luc Godard,* 13, 33.

49. Ibid., 40, 43.

50. Interview with Godard, *Cahiers du Cinéma.* Reprinted in Narboni and Milne, *Godard on Godard,* 172.

51. Jack Kerouac, *Desolation Angels* (1965; reprint, New York: Perigee Books, 1980), 280.

5. Constructing the Grotesque Body in Word, Image, and Sound

1. Mikhail Bakhtin, *Rabelais and His World,* trans. Hélène Iswolsky (Bloomington: Indiana University Press, 1984), 26.

2. Discussed in Ethan Spigland, "A Conversation with Raul Ruiz," *Persistence of Vision* 8 (1990): 72–84, cited at 79, 78.

3. Ibid., 73. This list of orifices excludes the anus, site of a production without use-value that Ruiz normally respects, in keeping with his critical view of commodity culture. He criticizes the Surrealists, for example, for wanting "to keep you busy even while you were asleep. It's a capitalistic problem. They wanted you to use your own dreams to make machines that can produce work, that can produce money or objects. It's an obsession with the production of culture" (80).

4. Ibid., 73.

5. John Tytell, *Naked Angels: The Lives & Literature of the Beat Generation* (New York: McGraw-Hill Book Company, 1976), 116, 118.

6. Gregory Stephenson, "The Gnostic Vision of William S. Burroughs," in *The Daybreak Boys: Essays on the Literature of the Beat Generation* (Carbondale: Southern Illinois University Press, 1990), 63.

7. See the analyses of this issue by Christian Metz in *Film Language: A Semiotics of the Cinema,* trans. Michael Taylor (New York: Oxford University Press, 1974), and in *Language and Cinema,* trans. Donna Jean Umiker-Sebeok (The Hague: Mouton, 1974).

8. Anne Friedberg, "'Cut-Ups': A *Syn*ema of the Text," in *William S. Burroughs at the Front: Critical Reception, 1959–1989,* ed. Jennie Skerl and Robin Lydenberg (Carbondale: Southern Illinois University Press, 1991), 171.

9. Stephenson, "Gnostic Vision of William S. Burroughs," 62. These agencies acquire their power from the prison-house nature of language. "We experience ourselves and the world through language, but language limits our experience to its implicit patterns. Our life within the limits of our language is our reality" (63).

10. Louis Althusser, "Ideology and Ideological State Apparatuses (Notes Towards an Investigation)," in *Video Culture: A Critical Investigation,* ed. John G. Hanhardt (Layton, Utah: Peregrine Smith Books, 1986), 56–95.

11. William S. Burroughs, *The Ticket That Exploded* (New York: Grove Press, 1987), 213.

12. William Burroughs, *Electronic Revolution* (Bonn: Expanded Media Editions, 1970), 57. Burroughs also describes the human body as "an image on screen talking." Burroughs, *Ticket That Exploded,* 178.

13. Tytell, *Naked Angels,* 120–21.

14. Edward Halsey Foster, *Understanding the Beats* (Columbia: University of South Carolina Press, 1992), 173.

15. Stephenson, "Gnostic Vision of William S. Burroughs," 63–64.

16. Rosalind Krauss, "Paul Sharits," *Film Culture* 65–66 (1978): 99. Krauss relates this "mentalizing" process to Surrealist film and to "cinema's exploration of the processes of association." While she applies the phrase specifically to Frampton's film *Poetic Justice,* it is equally relevant to *Zorns Lemma.* With regard to *T,O,U,C,H,I,N,G,* she calls the mentalizing process "in part the course to which Sharits wishes to refer," adding the qualifying phrase "in part" because she believes that the film is constructed as a "complex set of interlocking metaphors that are meant to combine to create a unified psychological field."

17. Frampton begins and ends *Zorns Lemma* with the flatness of the screen entirely blacked or whited out, and during the central segment he juxtaposes the relative flatness of motionless mise-en-scène (shots containing stationary printed words) with the contrasting three-dimensionality of shots with deeper fields. (The shots displaying printed words were originally made as still photographs, but Frampton subsequently decided to replace most of them with cinematic images precisely because he wanted them to display a greater depth of field.) Sharits contrasts flat frames (empty frames and frames displaying printed letters) with the limited but perceptible depth of figurative shots.

18. See P. Adams Sitney, *Visionary Film: The American Avant-Garde, 1943–1978* (New York: Oxford University Press, 1979), and Malcolm Le Grice, *Abstract Film and Beyond* (Cambridge: MIT Press, 1982). Two points about duration are worth mentioning here. A viewer who figures out the guiding principles of the long central portion of *Zorns Lemma* can estimate its duration with some accuracy even on a first viewing, and Frampton literally measures out the seconds of the film's last portion with a metronome. A catalogue listing for Sharits's film ironically acknowledges that for many spectators it may operate "at the limits" of not only "perception" but "possibly tolerance" as well. See the *Film-Makers' Cooperative Catalogue,* no. 7 (New York: Film-Makers' Cooperative, 1989), 433; the catalogue note quoted here is excerpted from an article by Simon Field in the *Monthly Film Bulletin,* London.

19. David E. James, *Allegories of Cinema: American Film in the Sixties* (Princeton: Princeton University Press, 1988), 240–44. The reference to "thrust and counterthrust" is quoted from Cleanth Brooks, an important figure in New Criticism.

20. Sharits quoted by Linda Cathcart, "An Interview with Paul Sharits," *Film Culture* 65–66 (1978): 106.

21. This does not mean it is without signification. Krauss relates its eye-cutting imagery and mood of explosive lust to Surrealist film (particularly Luis Buñuel's 1929 *Un Chien andalou*) and to cinema's frequent "exploration of the processes of association" (99). This insight links the dialectic of image and language in *T,O,U,C,H,I,N,G* to the history of psycho-

analytic thought, the interplay between image and language in dream interpretation, the relationships between dreamwork's primary and secondary processes, etc.

22. Paul Sharits, "Hearing : Seeing." *Film Culture* 65–66 (1978): 72.

23. Greil Marcus, *Lipstick Traces: A Secret History of the Twentieth Century* (Cambridge: Harvard University Press, 1989), 253; emphasis in original.

24. See, for example, the insert in *Film Culture* 65–66 (1978), characteristically entitled "'"hi" *hay yeh* folks, step' on in '&' transverse 'yr present' position." See also certain titles of his film works, such as *synchronousoundtracks* (1973–74), which Annette Michelson links with "concrete poetry" in "Paul Sharits and the Critique of Illusionism: An Introduction" *Film Culture* 65–66 (1978): 87.

25. Some of the documented alternates: it's gone, it's off, it's cut, his straw, history. Regina Cornwell, "Paul Sharits: Illusion and Object," in *Movies and Methods: An Anthology,* vol. 1, ed. Bill Nichols (Berkeley: University of California Press, 1976), 370.

26. See Paul Sharits, "Words per Page," *Film Culture* 65–66 (1978): 33.

27. Cornwell reports that some audience members fail to hear "destroy" at all; but most do hear it (for a while), and since that word is present by Sharits's own testimony, the listeners cited by Cornwell must be exceptions. See also the work of poet Jackson Mac Low, e.g., "Phoneme Dance."

28. "All through the film the word 'destroy' is repeated. . . . Eventually the ear refuses to register it, and it begins to sound like other words." Sitney, *Visionary Film,* 389. Whatever his accuracy regarding the phonic alteration, Sitney is wrong about the sound's ubiquity, since the central segment of the film is silent.

29. Paul Sharits, "—UR(i)N(ul)LS:TREAM:S:S:ECTION:S:SECTION:S:S:ECTIONED(A)(lysis)JO:'1968–70,'" *Film Culture* 65–66 (1978): 23.

30. Cornwell, "Paul Sharits," 372. This film, made in 1968–71 and known for short as *S:S:S:S:S:S,* also has a repeated and elusive word, transcribed in Sitney, *Visionary Film,* 389, as "exochorion." It is recorded in a fuguelike way and in what appear to be different phonemic combinations.

31. Sharits uses a similar strategy in *S:S:S:S:S:S,* which contains not only the "dam splices" already discussed but also handmade scratches on the film emulsion that are analogous with the photographed water flow and with the material presence of the filmstrip itself. As noted above, *S:S:S:S:S:S* also contains a rhythmically spoken word, more euphonious than that of *T,O,U,C,H,I,N,G* but given a similar degree of indeterminacy, although it does not "destroy itself" (Sharits's intention, as reported by Cornwell in "Paul Sharits," 370) in so reflexive and ironic a manner.

32. Marcus, *Lipstick Traces,* 248.

33. Michelson has linked "the passage from *cinema* to *film*" with a "detailed critique of illusionism." Michelson, "Paul Sharits and the Critique of Illusionism," 86; emphasis in original. See also Christian Metz's treatment of the terms *filmic* and *cinematic* in *Language and Cinema,* 51–52 and passim. Sharits himself has advocated the term *cinematics* to describe the orientation he prefers, but this is at least partly because it sounds less "clumsy" than a word like *filmatics.* See Paul Sharits, "A Cinematics Model for Film Studies in Higher Education," *Film Culture* 65–66 (1978): 67n. See also Sharits, "Words per Page."

34. Sharits, "Hearing : Seeing," 72.

35. An image-language dialectic also functions in some of Sharits's work after his flicker-film period, as in the excellent 1982 film installation *3rd Degree.* Yet he appears to be increasingly preoccupied with the power of the image, as *3rd Degree* illustrates with its highly ironic sound track featuring four words, "Look, I won't talk." This sentence is presented as the statement of a young woman apparently being threatened with torture, but it may also be read as a message addressed to the audience: Use your eyes, because communication by the spoken word is not what this work is about!

36. Hollis Frampton, *Circles of Confusion: Film-Photography-Video—Texts 1968–1980* (Rochester: Visual Studies Workshop Press, 1983), 114.

37. The title of a slightly later Frampton film, *Poetic Justice,* has been defined as "a figure of speech for irony." Allen S. Weiss, "*Poetic Justice:* Formations of Subjectivity and Sexual Identity," *Cinema Journal* 28, no. 1 (1988): 60.

38. Sitney, *Visionary Film,* 394.

39. In this section, there are also twenty-four "slots" available to be "filled" by word shots and (as the replacements proceed) nonword shots. This arrangement represents Frampton's clever blending of the alphabetic and chronographic ordering systems: The number twenty-four is derived from cinema's technological protocol of twenty-four frames per second, and it also represents the number of letters in the Roman alphabet, which subtracts two from the twenty-six-letter English alphabet by not distinguishing between *I* and *J* or between *U* and *V.*

40. James, *Allegories of Cinema,* 256–60. Frampton himself illuminated various textual, subtextual, paratextual, and extratextual issues related to *Zorns Lemma* in a particularly valuable interview conducted by Scott MacDonald in several sessions from 1976 to 1978; see Scott MacDonald, "Hollis Frampton," in *A Critical Cinema: Interviews with Independent Filmmakers* (Berkeley: University of California Press, 1987), 21–77.

41. Jean-Jacques Nattiez, *Music and Discourse: Toward a Semiology of Music,* trans. Carolyn Abbate (Princeton: Princeton University Press,

1990), 148. The last assertion has debatable implications about matters outside the range of my discussion.

42. Allen S. Weiss, "Cartesian Simulacra." *Persistence of Vision* 5 (spring 1987): 58. *Poetic Justice* consists almost entirely of shots of a screenplay's pages being placed onto a table one after another, allowing the spectator to see and read them.

43. Allen S. Weiss, "Music and Madness: Wolfson, Artaud, Wolfli," *Public* 4, no. 5 (1991): 100, 90.

44. For example, "Ah Pook the Destroyer/Brion Gysin's All-Purpose Bedtime Story" (Burroughs and Cale), on the CD recording by William S. Burroughs, *Dead City Radio* (Island 422–846 264–62).

45. For example, "Ich Bin von Kopf bis Fuss auf Liebe Eingestellt ('Falling in Love Again')" (Hollander), on Burroughs, *Dead City Radio.*

46. Its first public presentation was at the Guggenheim Museum, New York, in 1970, employing fifteen generations of the composer-performer's speech. The work was presented again in 1972 at the Brooklyn Academy of Music, New York, in a longer version designed to accompany a Viola Farber dance. It has also been presented by other musicians, including Lars-Gunnar Bodin, who presented a Swedish Radio version in 1979.

47. Alvin Lucier, *I Am Sitting in a Room,* Lovely Music–Vital Records VR-1013. Lucier made this definitive realization in 1980, employing thirty-two generations of speech and using his own living room as the sonic setting.

48. Ibid., liner notes.

49. Steve Reich, *It's Gonna Rain,* in *Early Works,* Elektra-Nonesuch 79-169-2, liner notes. It is instructive to contrast Reich's use of "found voice" material with that of Gavin Bryars in *Jesus' Blood Never Failed Me Yet,* in which an anonymous street singer's a capella voice is joined by an incrementally growing ensemble of accompanying instruments added by the composer in a studio; the effect is far more preservative in its effect and "classical" in its appeal than is the case in Reich's pieces.

50. Steve Reich, *Come Out,* in *Early Works.*

51. Steve Reich, *Different Trains,* Kronos Quartet, Elektra-Nonesuch 79176-2.

52. Scott Johnson, *John Somebody* and *No Memory,* in *John Somebody,* Nonesuch 79133. My quotations of Johnson are from the liner notes to this recording.

53. Philip Glass and Robert Wilson, *Einstein on the Beach,* the Philip Glass Ensemble and others, CBS Masterworks Records M4K 38875. An earlier recorded version, somewhat abridged and subtly different in tone and timbre at times, appeared on the Tomato label some years earlier. Excerpts from the opera appear on a number of Glass's other recordings.

54. Glass drew the distinction between the libretto and book of the opera in one of my interviews with him; by "book" he means something

like the book of a Broadway musical, which contains verbal material (dialogue, etc.) other than song lyrics.

55. Laurence Shyer uses the "language is a whore" remark by Burroughs, quoted above, to illustrate his point that Wilson has a "distrust of language" typical of "the experimental theatre of his generation, a movement deeply influenced by the writings of Antonin Artaud." Laurence Shyer, *Robert Wilson and His Collaborators* (New York: Theatre Communications Group, 1989), 90. In one of my interviews with Wilson, incidentally, he described the difficulty he was having in finding a publisher for "Typings"—a collection of Christopher Knowles's written work—who would present the material as a body of creative art rather than a curiosity produced by mental dysfunction.

INDEX

David Sterritt is film critic of the *Christian Science Monitor,* a professor of theater and film at the C. W. Post Campus of Long Island University, and a member of the film studies faculty at Columbia University. His essays and articles have appeared in the *New York Times,* the *Chronicle of Higher Education, Film Comment, Cineaste, Hitchcock Annual,* and many other periodicals, as well as numerous anthologies. He has written or edited *The Films of Alfred Hitchcock; The Films of Jean-Luc Godard: Seeing the Invisible; Mad to Be Saved: The Beats, the '50s, and Film;* and *Robert Altman: Interviews.* He served for several years on the selection committee of the New York Film Festival, has twice been elected chair of the New York Film Critics Circle, and is cochair of the Columbia University Seminar on Cinema and Interdisciplinary Interpretation.